PIPSQUEAKS

**Thirty five knitting designs for
babies and children up to ten years old**

Kim Hargreaves

ROWAN

First published in Great Britain in 2000 by
Rowan Yarns Ltd
Green Lane Mill
Holmfirth
West Yorkshire
England
HD7 1RW

Designs & Styling Kim Hargreaves
Photographer Joey Toller
Hair & Make-up Mark Thompson
Book Design Kim Hargreaves
Design Co-ordinator Kathleen Hargreaves
Design Layout Les Dunford
Knitting co-ordinators Elizabeth Armitage & Lyndsay Kaye
Pattern writers Stella Smith & Sue Whiting

British Library Cataloguing in Publication Data
Rowan Yarns
Pipsqueaks
1. Knitting – patterns
1 Title
ISBN 0 9525375 0 5

Printed by KHL Printing Co Pte Ltd
Singapore

Contents

Left Scamp knitted in Handknit DK Cotton, this page Maisie knitted in 4 Ply Cotton

This page Core, right Hero both knitted in Rowan Denim

Left Sweet knitted in Cotton Glace, this page Sport knitted in Handknit DK Cotton   9

Left Lucky knitted in All Seasons Cotton, this page Cheesecake knitted in Cotton Glace

Left Scamp knitted in Rowan Denim, this page Nixon knitted in Wool Cotton

Left Imp knitted in Cotton Glace, this page Archie knitted in Cotton Glace

Left Jolly, this page Strawberry both knitted in True 4 ply Botany

This page Mimi knitted in 4 ply Cotton, right Daisy knitted in Cotton Glace

Chill knitted in DK Soft

22 *This page Harry knitted in All Seasons Cotton, right Mickey knitted in 4 Ply Cotton*

*Left Crumpet knitted in Chunky Tweed & Squiffy knitted in DK Soft,
this page Sweet and Squiffy both knitted in DK Soft*

Billie knitted in Wool Cotton

Left Muffin knitted in DK Soft, this page Pumpkin knitted in Wool Cotton

Left Action knitted in Handknit DK Cotton, this page Strike knitted in Wool Cotton

This page Fletcher knitted in All Seasons Cotton, right Angel knitted in Wool Cotton

Left Twinkle knitted in 4 Ply Cotton, this page Mimi knitted in 4 Ply Cotton and Fletcher knitted in All Seasons Cotton

35

This page Action knitted in Handknit DK Cotton, right Harry knitted in All Seasons Cotton

This page Billie knitted in Wool Cotton, opposite Chill knitted in DK Soft 39

This page Scamp knitted in Rowan Denim, opposite Mickey knitted in 4 ply Cotton

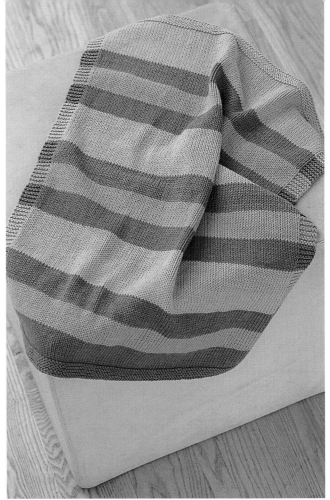

Flump & Munchie both knitted in All Seasons Cotton

Peaches knitted in Handknit DK Cotton

Cheesecake knitted in Cotton Glace

Lucky

Crumpet & Squiffy

Chill

Hide Cushions & Blanket all knitted in DK Soft

Mushroom knitted in All Seasons Cotton

THE KNITTING PATTERNS

The designs in this magazine are all sized according to Kim's original inspiration and are graded accordingly. All of the garments are photographed on the correct size child; to help you to decide which size to knit we have numbered the sizes throughout the magazine to help you translate garments with the correct fit onto your child. To facilitate this there is a size diagram included with each pattern which shows not only the finished garment length and width but will also enable you to calculate the crucial centre-back to cuff measurement needed to ensure a perfect fit.

Design number 1

Nixon

YARN
Rowan Wool Cotton

		5th	6th	7th	8th	9th	
To fit		3-4	4-5	6-7	8-9	9-10	yrs
Chest size		23	24	26	28	30in	
		58	61	66	71	76cm)	
A Antique	900	4	4	5	5	6 x 50gm	
B Inky	908	2	2	2	3	3 x 50gm	

NEEDLES
1 pair 3¾mm (no 9) (US 5) needles
1 pair 4mm (no 8) (US 6) needles

TENSION
22 sts and 30 rows to 10 cm measured over stocking stitch using 4mm (US 6) needles.

BACK and FRONT (both alike)
Cast on 72 (78: 86: 94: 100) sts using 3¾mm (US 5) needles and yarn A.

Row 1 (RS): Using yarn A P0 (1: 0: 0: 0), K2 (4: 3: 1: 4), ★P2, K4, rep from ★ to last 4 (1: 5: 3: 0) sts, P2 (1: 2: 2: 0), K2 (0: 3: 1: 0).
Row 2: Using yarn A K0 (1: 0: 0: 0), P2 (4: 3: 1: 4), ★K2, P4, rep from ★ to last 4 (1: 5: 3: 0) sts, K2 (1: 2: 2: 0), P2 (0: 3: 1: 0).
Rows 3 and 4: As rows 1 and 2.
Rows 5 and 6: As rows 1 and 2 but using yarn B.
Rows 7 to 10: As rows 1 and 2, twice.
Change to 4mm (US 6) needles and cont in st st as folls:
Row 1 (RS): Using yarn B knit.
Row 2: Using yarn B purl.
Row 3: Using yarn A knit.
Row 4: Using yarn A purl.
Rows 5 and 6: As rows 3 and 4.
Cont straight in striped st st as set until work measures 17 (18.5: 20: 22: 23) cm, ending with a WS row.
Shape armholes
Cast off 6 sts at beg of next 2 rows.
60 (66: 74: 82: 88) sts.
Cont straight until armhole measures 12.5 (13.5: 14.5: 15.5: 16.5) cm, ending with a WS row.
Break off yarn B and cont using yarn A only.
Change to 3¾mm (US 5) needles.
Next row (RS): P0 (1: 0: 0: 0), K2 (4: 3: 1: 4), ★P2, K4, rep from ★ to last 4 (1: 5: 3: 0) sts, P2 (1: 2: 2: 0), K2 (0: 3: 1: 0).
Next row: K0 (1: 0: 0: 0), P2 (4: 3: 1: 4), ★K2, P4, rep from ★ to last 4 (1: 5: 3: 0) sts, K2 (1: 2: 2: 0), P2 (0: 3: 1: 0).
Cont in rib as set until armhole measures 16 (17: 18: 19: 20) cm, ending with a WS row.
Cast off in rib.

SLEEVES (both alike)
Cast on 36 (38: 40: 42: 44) sts using 3¾mm (US 5) needles and yarn A and work in striped rib as folls:
Row 1 (RS): Using yarn A K0 (0: 1: 2: 3), P1 (2: 2: 2: 2), ★K4, P2, rep from ★ to last 5 (0: 1: 2: 3) sts, K4 (0: 1: 2: 3), P1 (0: 0: 0: 0).
Row 2: Using yarn A P0 (0: 1: 2: 3), K1 (2: 2: 2: 2), ★P4, K2, rep from ★ to last 5 (0: 1: 2: 3) sts, P4 (0: 1: 2: 3), K1 (0: 0: 0: 0).
Rows 3 and 4: As rows 1 and 2.

Row 5: As row 1 but using yarn B.
Row 6: As row 2 but using yarn B.
Change to 4mm (US 6) needles.
Cont in striped rib as set, inc 1 st at each end of next and every foll 6th row to 44 (50: 56: 66: 74) sts, then on every foll 4th row until there are 70 (74: 80: 84: 88) sts, taking inc sts into rib.
Cont straight until sleeve measures 29.5 (32.5: 36.5: 40: 43.5) cm from cast-on edge, ending with a WS row.
Cast off in rib.

MAKING UP
PRESS all pieces as described on the information page.
Join shoulder seams using back stitch, leaving 18 (19: 20: 21: 22) cm open at centre for neck opening.
See information page for finishing instructions, setting in sleeves using the square set-in method.

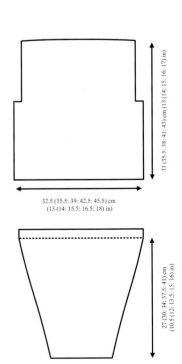

33 (35.5: 38: 41: 43) cm (13 (14: 15: 16: 17) in)

32.5 (35.5: 39: 42.5: 45.5) cm
(13 (14: 15.5: 16.5: 18) in)

27 (30: 34: 37.5: 41) cm
(10.5 (12: 13.5: 15: 16) in)

Pumpkin

YARN

Rowan Wool Cotton

	1st	2nd	
To fit	0-6	6-12	mths
Chest size	16	18	in
	(41	46	cm)
	3	4	x 50gm

(photographed in Rich 911)

3rd	4th	5th	6th	7th	8th	9th	
To fit							
1-2	2-3	3-4	4-5	6-7	8-9	9-10 yrs	
Chest size							
20	22	23	24	26	28	30	in
(51	56	58	61	66	71	76	cm)
5	6	7	9	10	12	13	x 50gm

NEEDLES

1 pair 3¼mm (no 10) (US 3) needles
1 pair 4mm (no 8) (US 6) needles

BUTTONS - 2

TENSION

22 sts and 30 rows to 10 cm measured over stocking stitch using 4mm (US 6) needles.

BACK

Cast on 57 (65: 73: 81: 89: 95: 101: 111: 123) sts using 3¼mm (US 3) needles.
Knit 3 rows.
Row 4 (WS): K1, *P1, K1, rep from * to end.
Row 5: As row 4.
Rows 4 and 5 form moss st.
Work a further 3 (3: 3: 5: 5: 5: 7: 7: 7) rows in moss st, ending with a WS row.
Change to 4mm (US 6) needles and, beg with a K row, cont in st st as folls:
Work straight until back measures 11.5 (15: 18: 21.5: 25.5: 28: 30.5: 35.5: 38) cm, ending with a WS row.
Shape armholes
Cast off 4 (4: 4: 5: 5: 5: 6: 6: 6) sts at beg of next 2 rows. 49 (57: 65: 71: 79: 85: 89: 99: 111) sts.
Cont straight until armhole measures 11.5 (13: 15: 16.5: 17.5: 19: 20: 21.5: 23) cm, ending with a WS row.
Shape shoulders and back neck
Cast off 4 (5: 6: 6: 8: 8: 9: 10: 12) sts at beg of

next 2 rows. 41 (47: 53: 59: 63: 69: 71: 79: 87) sts.
Next row (RS): Cast off 4 (5: 6: 6: 8: 8: 9: 10: 12) sts, K until there are 7 (8: 9: 11: 11: 13: 12: 14: 15) sts on right needle and turn, leaving rem sts on a holder.
Work each side of neck separately.
Cast off 4 sts at beg of next row.
Cast off rem 3 (4: 5: 7: 7: 9: 8: 10: 11) sts.
With RS facing, rejoin yarn to rem sts, cast off centre 19 (21: 23: 25: 25: 27: 29: 31: 33) sts, K to end.
Work to match first side, reversing shapings.

FRONT

Work as for back until armhole measures 3.5 (4: 6: 6.5: 7.5: 8: 9: 9.5: 11)cm, ending with a WS row.
Divide for front opening
Next row (RS): K22 (26: 30: 33: 37: 39: 41: 46: 52), (K1, P1) 2 (2: 2: 2: 2: 3: 3: 3: 3) times, K1 and turn, leaving rem sts on a holder.
Work each side of neck separately.
Next row (WS): (K1, P1) 2 (2: 2: 2: 2: 3: 3: 3: 3) times, K1, P to end.
27 (31: 35: 38: 42: 46: 48: 53: 59) sts.
This row sets 5 (5: 5: 5: 5: 7: 7: 7: 7) front opening edge sts now worked in moss st.
Keeping border correct as set, cont straight until front matches back to start of shoulder shaping, ending with a WS row.
Shape shoulder
Cast off 4 (5: 6: 6: 8: 8: 9: 10: 12) sts at beg of next and foll alt row, then 3 (4: 5: 7: 7: 9: 8: 10: 11) sts at beg of foll alt row.
Work 1 row on rem 16 (17: 18: 19: 19: 21: 22: 23: 24) sts.
Break yarn and leave sts on a holder.
With RS facing, rejoin yarn to rem sts, cast on 5 (5: 5: 5: 5: 7: 7: 7: 7) sts, (K1, P1) 2 (2: 2: 2: 2: 3: 3: 3: 3) times, K1 across these 5 (5: 5: 5: 5: 7: 7: 7: 7) sts, then K to end.
27 (31: 35: 38: 42: 46: 48: 53: 59) sts.
Next row (WS): P to last 5 (5: 5: 5: 5: 7: 7: 7: 7) sts, (K1, P1) 2 (2: 2: 2: 2: 3: 3: 3: 3) times, K1.
This row sets 5 (5: 5: 5: 5: 7: 7: 7: 7) front opening edge sts now worked in moss st.
Keeping border correct as set, cont straight until front matches back to start of shoulder shaping, ending with a RS row.
Shape shoulder
Cast off 4 (5: 6: 6: 8: 8: 9: 10: 12) sts at beg of next and foll alt row, then 3 (4: 5: 7: 7: 9: 8: 10: 11) sts at beg of foll alt row.
Do NOT break yarn.
Leave rem 16 (17: 18: 19: 19: 21: 22: 23: 24) sts on a holder and set aside ball of yarn – this will be used for hood.

SLEEVES (both alike)

Cast on 33 (37: 39: 41: 45: 47: 51: 53: 55) sts using 3¼mm (US 3) needles.
Knit 3 rows.
Work 3 (3: 3: 5: 5: 5: 7: 7: 7) rows in moss st as given for back, ending with a WS row.
Change to 4mm (US 6) needles and, beg with a K row, cont in st st, inc 1 st at each end of next and every foll alt (4th: alt: alt: alt: 4th: 4th: 4th: 4th) row to 39 (53: 49: 49: 49: 81: 79: 87: 93) sts, then on every foll 4th (6th: 4th: 4th: 4th: 6th: 6th: 6th: 6th) row until there are 51 (57: 67: 73: 77: 83: 89: 95: 101) sts.
Cont straight until sleeve measures 14.5 (18.5: 20: 24: 25.5: 28.5: 33.5: 36: 38.5) cm, ending with a WS row.
Cast off loosely.

MAKING UP

PRESS all pieces as described on the information page.
Join shoulder seams using back stitch.
Hood
With RS facing, using ball of yarn left at right front neck edge and 4mm (US 6) needles, patt across 16 (17: 18: 19: 19: 21: 22: 23: 24) sts of right front as folls: (K1, P1) to last 0 (1: 0: 1: 1: 1: 0: 1: 0) st, K0 (1: 0: 1: 1: 1: 0: 1: 0), pick up and knit 27 (29: 31: 33: 33: 35: 37: 39: 41) sts across back neck placing marker on centre st, then patt across 16 (17: 18: 19: 19: 21: 22: 23: 24) sts of left front as folls: K0 (1: 0: 1: 1: 1: 0: 1: 0), (P1, K1) to end. 59 (63: 67: 71: 71: 77: 81: 85: 89) sts.
Working all sts in moss st as set by front neck sts, cont as folls:
Work 7 rows.
Next row (RS) (inc): Moss st to marked st, M1, K1, M1, moss st to end.
Rep last 8 rows once more.
63 (67: 71: 75: 75: 81: 85: 89: 93) sts.
Cont straight until hood measures 19 (20: 21: 22: 23: 24: 25: 26: 27) cm, ending with a WS row.
Next row (RS) (dec): Moss st to within 2 sts of marked st, work 2 tog, K1, work 2 tog tbl, moss st to end.
Work 1 row.
Rep last 2 rows twice more, dec 1 st at centre of last row. 56 (60: 64: 68: 68: 74: 78: 82: 86) sts.
Next row (RS): Patt 28 (30: 32: 34: 34: 37: 39: 41: 43) sts and turn.
Fold hood in half with WS facing and, using a spare needle, cast off sts from each needle tog to form hood seam.
Button loops (make 2)
Cast on 14 sts using 3¼mm (US 3) needles.
Cast off.
Lay one front border over the other and sew cast-on edge in place on inside. Fold button loops in half and sew to inside of front opening edge as in photograph. Attach buttons to correspond.
See information page for finishing instructions, setting in sleeves using the square set-in method.

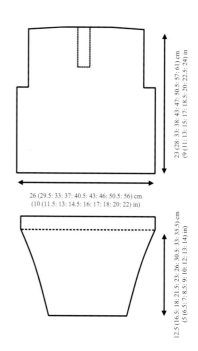

26 (29.5: 33: 37: 40.5: 43: 46: 50.5: 56) cm
(10 (11.5: 13: 14.5: 16: 17: 18: 20: 22) in)

23 (28: 33: 38: 43: 47: 50.5: 57: 61) cm
(9 (11: 13: 15: 17: 18.5: 20: 22.5: 24) in)

12.5 (16.5: 18: 21.5: 23: 26: 30.5: 33: 35.5) cm
(5 (6.5: 7: 8.5: 9: 10: 12: 13: 14) in)

Design number 3

Sweet

YARN

	6th	7th	8th	9th	
To fit	4-5	6-7	8-9	9-10	yrs
Chest size	24	26	28	30	in
	(61	66	71	76	cm)
Rowan Cotton Glace					
A	6	7	8	9 x 50gm	
B	1	1	1	1 x 50gm	

(cardigan photographed in Pixie 723 and Steel 798)
Rowan DK Soft

		4	4	5	5 x 50gm

(Sweater photographed in Tawny 171)

NEEDLES
Cotton Glace version
1 pair 2¾mm (no 12) (US 2) needles
1 pair 3¼mm (no 10) (US 3) needles
DK Soft version
1 pair 3¼mm (no 10) (US 3) needles
1 pair 4mm (no 8) (US 6) needles

BUTTONS - 7 for cardigan

TENSION
23 sts and 32 rows to 10 cm measured over stocking stitch using larger size needles - 3¼mm (US 3) for Cotton Glace or 4mm (US 6) for DK Soft.

Cardigan
(can be knitted in either Cotton Glace or DK Soft)
BACK
Cast on 313 (345: 377: 401) sts using smaller size needles and yarn B.
Break off yarn B and join in yarn A.
Work frill as folls:
Row 1 (RS): K1, ★K2, lift first of these 2 sts over 2nd st and off right needle, rep from ★ to end.
Row 2: P1, ★P2tog, rep from ★ to end.
These 2 rows complete frill. 79 (87: 95: 101) sts.
Change to larger size needles.
Starting and ending rows as indicated and repeating the 24 row patt repeat throughout, cont in patt from chart as folls:
Work 6 rows.
Dec 1 st at each end of next and every foll 6th row until 69 (77: 83: 89) sts rem.
Work 9 rows.
Inc 1 st at each end of next and every foll 6th (8th: 6th: 6th) row until there are 79 (87: 95: 101) sts, taking inc sts into patt.
Cont straight until back measures 24 (26: 28: 29) cm from lower edge, ending with a WS row.
Shape armholes
Keeping patt correct, cast off 4 sts at beg of next 2 rows. 71 (79: 87: 93) sts.
Dec 1 st at each end of next 5 rows, then on foll 1 (1: 3: 3) alt rows. 59 (67: 71: 77) sts.
Cont straight until armhole measures 16 (16: 17: 18) cm, ending with a WS row.
Shape shoulders and back neck
Cast off 5 (6: 7: 7) sts at beg of next 2 rows. 49 (55: 57: 63) sts.
Next row (RS): Cast off 5 (6: 7: 7) sts, patt until there are 10 (11: 10: 12) sts on right needle and turn, leaving rem sts on a holder.
Work each side of neck separately.
Cast off 4 sts at beg of next row.
Cast off rem 6 (7: 6: 8) sts.
With RS facing, rejoin yarn to rem sts, cast off centre 19 (21: 23: 25) sts, patt to end.
Work to match first side, reversing shapings.

LEFT FRONT
Cast on 157 (173: 189: 201) sts using smaller size needles and yarn B.
Break off yarn B and join in yarn A.
Work frill as folls:
Row 1 (RS): K1, ★K2, lift first of these 2 sts over 2nd st and off right needle, rep from ★ to end.
Row 2: P1, ★P2tog, rep from ★ to end.
These 2 rows complete frill. 40 (44: 48: 51) sts.
Change to larger size needles. Starting and ending rows as indicated and repeating the 24 row patt repeat throughout, cont in patt from chart, omitting any incomplete eyelets at centre front, as folls:
Work 6 rows.
Dec 1 st at beg of next and every foll 6th row until 35 (39: 42: 45) sts rem.
Work 9 rows.
Inc 1 st at beg of next and every foll 6th (8th: 6th: 6th) row until there are 40 (44: 48: 51) sts, taking inc sts into patt.
Cont straight until left front matches back to beg of armhole shaping, ending with a WS row.
Shape armhole
Keeping patt correct, cast off 4 sts at beg of next row. 36 (40: 44: 47) sts.
Work 1 row.
Dec 1 st at armhole edge of next 5 rows, then on foll 1 (1: 3: 3) alt rows. 30 (34: 36: 39) sts.
Cont straight until 11 (11: 13: 13) rows less have been worked than on back to start of shoulder shaping, ending with a RS row.

Shape neck
Cast off 9 (10: 10: 11) sts at beg of next row. 21 (24: 26: 28) sts.
Dec 1 st at neck edge of next 3 rows, then on foll 2 (2: 3: 3) alt rows. 16 (19: 20: 22) sts.
Work 3 rows, ending with a WS row.
Shape shoulder
Cast off 5 (6: 7: 7) sts at beg of next and foll alt row.
Work 1 row.
Cast off rem 6 (7: 6: 8) sts.

RIGHT FRONT
Cast on 157 (173: 189: 201) sts using smaller size needles and yarn B.
Break off yarn B and join in yarn A.
Work frill as folls:
Row 1 (RS): K1, ★K2, lift first of these 2 sts over 2nd st and off right needle, rep from ★ to end.
Row 2: P1, ★P2tog, rep from ★ to end.
These 2 rows complete frill. 40 (44: 48: 51) sts.
Change to larger size needles.
Starting and ending rows as indicated and repeating the 24 row patt repeat throughout, cont in patt from chart, omitting any incomplete eyelets at centre front, as folls:
Work 6 rows.
Dec 1 st at end of next and every foll 6th row until 35 (39: 42: 45) sts rem.
Complete to match left front, reversing shapings.

SLEEVES (both alike)
Cast on 145 (153: 161: 169) sts using smaller size needles and yarn B.
Break off yarn B and join in yarn A.
Work frill as folls:
Row 1 (RS): K1, ★K2, lift first of these 2 sts over 2nd st and off right needle, rep from ★ to end.
Row 2: P1, ★P2tog, rep from ★ to end.
These 2 rows complete frill. 37 (39: 41: 43) sts.
Change to larger size needles.
Starting and ending rows as indicated and rep the 24 row patt repeat throughout, cont in patt from chart, shaping sides by inc 1 st at each end of 9th and every foll 8th row to 43 (47: 51: 61) sts, then on every foll 6th row until there are 63 (67: 71: 73) sts, taking inc sts into patt.
Cont straight until sleeve measures 30.5 (33: 35.5: 38) cm from lower edge, ending with a WS row.
Shape top
Keeping patt correct, cast off 4 sts at beg of next 2 rows. 55 (59: 63: 65) sts.
Dec 1 st at each end of next 3 rows, then on foll 2 (3: 2: 3) alt rows. 45 (47: 53: 53) sts.
Work 3 rows.
Dec 1 st at each end of next and every foll 4th row until 39 (43: 45: 45) sts rem, then on every foll alt row until 35 (35: 39: 39) sts rem.
Dec 1 st at each end of next 3 rows, ending with a WS row. 29 (29: 33: 33) sts.
Cast off 4 sts at beg of next 2 rows.
Cast off rem 21 (21: 25: 25) sts.

MAKING UP
PRESS all pieces as described on the info page.
Join shoulder seams using back stitch.
Button border
With RS facing, yarn A and smaller size needles, pick up and knit 88 (95: 102: 109) sts along left front opening edge.
Beg with a **knit** row, work 4 rows in rev st st.
Cast off knitwise (on WS).
Buttonhole border
Please note the buttonholes are made on the pick-up row and are worked as folls:
With RS facing, yarn A and smaller size needles,

pick up and knit 11 (12: 13: 14) sts, *cast off next 2 sts (leaving one st on needle after buttonhole), pick up and knit a further 9 (10: 11: 12) sts, rep from * 5 times more, cast off next 2 sts, pick up and knit a further 2 sts.
88 (95: 102: 109) sts.
Row 1 (WS): Knit to end, working (yfwd) twice over each pair of sts cast-off on pick up row.
Row 2: Purl to end, working into back of each yfwd of previous row.
Beg with a **knit** row, work a further 2 rows in rev st st.
Cast off knitwise (on WS).
Neck border
With RS facing, yarn A and smaller size needles, starting and ending halfway across top of borders, pick up and knit 23 (24: 27: 28) sts up right side of neck, 27 (29: 31: 33) sts from back neck, and 23 (24: 27: 28) sts down left side of neck.
73 (77: 85: 89) sts.
Beg with a **knit** row, work 4 rows in rev st st.
Cast off knitwise (on WS).
See information page for finishing instructions, setting in sleeves using the set-in method.

Sweater
(can be knitted in either DK Soft or Cotton Glace)
BACK
Cast on 313 (345: 377: 401) sts using smaller size needles.
Work frill as folls:
Row 1 (RS): K1, *K2, lift first of these 2 sts over 2nd st and off right needle, rep from * to end.
Row 2: P1, *P2tog, rep from * to end.
These 2 rows complete frill. 79 (87: 95: 101) sts.
Change to larger size needles.
Beg with a K row, cont in st st as folls:
Work 6 rows.
Dec 1 st at each end of next and every foll 6th row until 69 (77: 83: 89) sts rem.
Work 9 rows.
Inc 1 st at each end of next and every foll 6th (8th: 6th: 6th) row until there are 79 (87: 95: 101) sts.
Cont straight until back measures 24 (26: 28: 29) cm from lower edge, ending with a WS row.
Shape armholes
Cast off 4 sts at beg of next 2 rows.
71 (79: 87: 93) sts.
Dec 1 st at each end of next 5 rows, then on foll 1 (1: 3: 3) alt rows. 59 (67: 71: 77) sts.
Cont straight until armhole measures

16 (16: 17: 18) cm, ending with a WS row.
Shape shoulders and back neck
Cast off 5 (6: 6: 7) sts at beg of next 2 rows.
49 (55: 59: 63) sts.
Next row (RS): Cast off 5 (6: 6: 7) sts, K until there are 9 (10: 11: 11) sts on right needle and turn, leaving rem sts on a holder.
Work each side of neck separately.
Cast off 4 sts at beg of next row.
Cast off rem 5 (6: 7: 7) sts.
With RS facing, rejoin yarn to rem sts, cast off centre 21 (23: 25: 27) sts, K to end.
Work to match first side, reversing shapings.

FRONT
Work as for back until 14 (14: 16: 16) rows less have been worked than on back to start of shoulder shaping, ending with a WS row.
Shape neck
Next row (RS): K20 (23: 25: 27) and turn, leaving rem sts on a holder.
Work each side of neck separately.
Dec 1 st at neck edge of next 3 rows, then on foll 2 (2: 3: 3) alt rows. 15 (18: 19: 21) sts.
Work 6 rows.
Shape shoulder
Cast off 5 (6: 6: 7) sts at beg of next and foll alt row.
Work 1 row.
Cast off rem 5 (6: 7: 7) sts.
With RS facing, rejoin yarn to rem sts, cast off centre 19 (21: 21: 23) sts, K to end.
Work to match first side, reversing shapings.

SLEEVES (both alike)
Cast on 145 (153: 161: 169) sts using smaller size needles.
Work frill as folls:
Row 1 (RS): K1, *K2, lift first of these 2 sts over 2nd st and off right needle, rep from * to end.
Row 2: P1, *P2tog, rep from * to end.
These 2 rows complete frill. 37 (39: 41: 43) sts.
Change to larger size needles.
Beg with a K row, cont in st st, shaping sides by inc 1 st at each end of 9th and every foll 8th row to 43 (47: 51: 61) sts, then on every foll 6th row until there are 63 (67: 71: 73) sts.
Cont straight until sleeve measures 30.5 (33: 35.5: 38) cm from lower edge, ending with a WS row.
Shape top
Cast off 4 sts at beg of next 2 rows.
55 (59: 63: 65) sts.

Dec 1 st at each end of next 3 rows, then on foll 2 (3: 2: 3) alt rows. 45 (47: 53: 53) sts.
Work 3 rows.
Dec 1 st at each end of next and every foll 4th row until 39 (43: 45: 45) sts rem, then on every foll alt row until 35 (35: 39: 39) sts rem.
Dec 1 st at each end of next 3 rows, ending with a WS row. 29 (29: 33: 33) sts.
Cast off 4 sts at beg of next 2 rows.
Cast off rem 21 (21: 25: 25) sts.

MAKING UP
PRESS all pieces as described on the info page.
Join right shoulder seam using back stitch.
Neck border
With RS facing and smaller size needles, pick up and knit 15 (15: 17: 17) sts down left front neck, 19 (21: 21: 23) sts across front neck, 15 (15: 17: 17) sts up right front neck, and 29 (31: 33: 35) sts across back neck. 78 (82: 88: 92) sts.
Beg with a **knit** row, work 4 rows in rev st st.
Cast off knitwise (on WS).
See information page for finishing instructions, setting in sleeve using the set-in method.

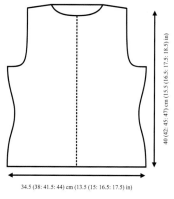

34.5 (38: 41.5: 44) cm (13.5 (15: 16.5: 17.5) in)

40 (42: 45: 47) cm (15.5 (16.5: 17.5: 18.5) in)

30.5 (33: 35.5: 38) cm (12 (13: 14: 15) in)

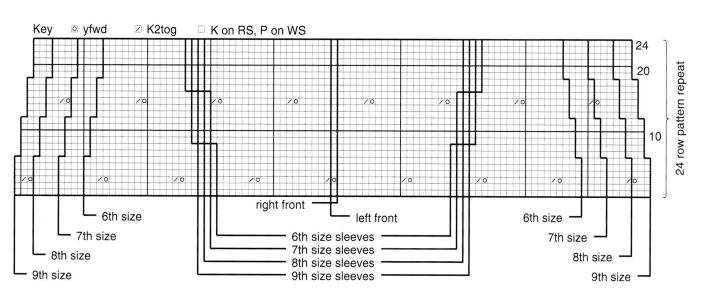

Key ⊙ yfwd ☑ K2tog ☐ K on RS, P on WS

24 row pattern repeat

6th size
7th size
8th size
9th size

right front   left front

6th size sleeves
7th size sleeves
8th size sleeves
9th size sleeves

6th size
7th size
8th size
9th size

Design number 4

Mickey

YARN

Rowan 4 ply Cotton

	1st	2nd	3rd		
To fit	0-6	6-12 mths	1-2 yrs		
Chest size	16	18	20	in	
	(41	46	51	cm)	
A Black 101	2	3	4	x	50gm
B Tear 116	1	1	1	x	50gm

NEEDLES

1 pair 2¾mm (no 12) (US 2) needles
1 pair 3 mm (no 11) (US 2/3) needles

BUTTONS – 4 (6: 6)

TENSION

28 sts and 36 rows to 10 cm measured over st st
using 3 mm (US 2/3) needles.

BACK

Cast on 69 (81: 93) sts using 2¾mm (US 2)
needles and yarn A.
Beg with a K row, work 6 rows in st st
Next row (RS): K3, ★ P3, K3, rep from ★ to end.
Next row: P3, ★ K3, P3, rep from ★ to end.
These 2 rows form rib.
Work a further 4 (6: 8) rows in rib.
Change to 3 mm (US 2/3) needles and, beg
with a K row, work in st st until back measures
11.5 (15: 18) cm, ending with a WS row.
Shape armholes
Cast off 5 sts at beg of next 2 rows.
59 (71: 83) sts.
Cont straight until armhole measures 8 (9.5: 13)
cm, ending with a WS row.
Change to 2¾mm (US 2) needles and cont in
K3, P3, rib for back yoke as folls:
Next row (RS): K4, ★ P3, K3, rep from ★ to
last st, K1.
Next row: K1, ★ P3, K3, rep from ★ to last 4 sts,
P3, K1.
Cont in rib as set until work measures
11.5 (13: 15) cm from beg of armhole shaping,
ending with a WS row.
Shape shoulders and back neck
Next row: Rib 14 (19: 23) sts and turn, leaving
rem sts on a holder.
Work each side of neck separately.

Cont on these sts, work a further 5 rows in rib as
set.
Cast off evenly in rib.
With RS facing, rejoin yarn to rem sts, cast off
centre 31 (33: 37) sts, rib to end.
Work a further 5 rows in rib on these sts. Cast off.

FRONT

Work as given for back until 2 (10: 20) rows of
st st have been completed, ending with a WS row.
Join in yarn B and place motif as folls:
Next row (RS): K14 (20: 26), starting with
chart row 1 and using the INTARSIA method
as described on the information page, work
across 42 sts from chart, K13 (19: 25).
Next row: P13 (19: 25), work across 42 sts from
chart, P14 (20: 26).
Cont working from chart until front matches back
to beg of armhole shaping, ending with a WS row.
Shape armholes
Keeping patt correct, cast off 5 sts at beg of next
2 rows. 59 (71: 83) sts.
Cont straight until chart row 61 has been
completed.
Break yarn B and cont using yarn A only.
Work straight until armhole measures 8 (9.5: 13) cm,
ending with a WS row.
Change to 2¾mm (US 2) needles and, beg with
a RS row, cont in K3, P3 rib as given for back
yoke until work measures 11.5 (13: 15) cm from
beg of armhole shaping, ending with a WS row.
Shape shoulders and front neck
Next row: Rib 14 (19: 23) sts and turn, leaving
rem sts on a holder.
Work each side of neck separately.
Cont on these sts, work 1 row in rib as set.
Next row (buttonhole row): Rib 4 (3: 7), ★
yrn, rib 2tog, rib 4, rep from ★ to last 4 sts, yrn,
rib 2tog, rib 2.
Work a further 3 rows in rib.
Cast off evenly in rib.
With RS facing, rejoin yarn to rem sts, cast off
centre 31 (33: 37) sts, rib to end.
Work 1 row in rib.
Next row (buttonhole row) : Rib 2, ★ rib
2tog, yrn, rib 4, rep from ★ to last 6 (5: 9) sts, rib
2 tog, yrn, rib to end.

Work a further 3 rows in rib as set.
Cast off evenly in rib.

SLEEVES (both alike)

Cast on 42 (45: 48) sts using 2¾mm (US 2)
needles and yarn A.
Work 6 rows in st st, ending with a WS row.
Beg with a RS row, work 6 (6: 8) rows in rib as
given for back, inc 1 (2: 1) sts at end(s) of last
row. 43 (47: 49) sts.
Change to 3 mm (US 2/3) needles.
Beg with a K row, work in st st, shaping sleeve
seam by inc 1 st at each end of 3rd and every
foll 4th row to 57 (71: 67) sts, then on every alt
row to 65 (73: 85) sts.
Cont without further shaping until sleeve measures
14.5 (18.5: 20) cm, ending with a WS row.
Cast off evenly.

MAKING UP

PRESS all pieces as described on the info page.
Overlap front buttonhole rib over back rib and
catch together row ends at side edges.
Set sleeve into armhole using the square set-in
method described on the information page.
Sew on buttons to correspond with buttonholes.
See information page for finishing instructions.

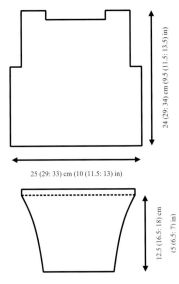

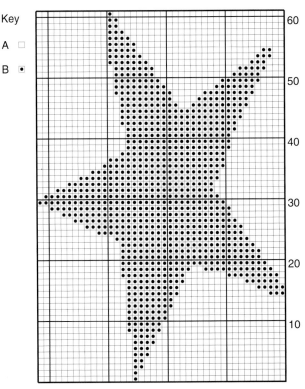

Key

A □

B ⊡

Core

YARN
Rowan Denim

	7th	8th	9th	
To fit	6-7	8-9	9-10	yrs
Chest size	26	28	30	in
	(66	71	76	cm)
	10	11	12	x 50gm

(photographed in Nashville 225)

NEEDLES
1 pair 3¼mm (no 10) (US 3) needles
1 pair 4mm (no 8) (US 6) needles

BUTTONS - 9

TENSION
Before washing 20 sts and 28 rows to 10 cm measured over stocking stitch using 4mm (US 6) needles.

Tension note: Denim will shrink in length when washed for the first time. Allowances have been made in this pattern for shrinkage (see size diagram for after washing measurements).

BACK
Cast on 67 (75: 79) sts using 3¼mm (US 3) needles.
Row 1 (RS): P1, *K1, P1, rep from * to end.
Row 2: As row 1.
These 2 rows form moss st.
Work a further 6 rows in moss st.
Change to 4mm (US 6) needles.
Next row (RS): P15 (17: 19), K2, P1, moss st 5, P1, K2, P15 (19: 19), K2, P1, moss st 5, P1, K2, P15 (17: 19).
Next row: K15 (17: 19), P2, K1, moss st 5, K1, P2, K15 (19: 19), P2, K1, moss st 5, K1, P2, K15 (17: 19).
Rep last 2 rows 8 (8: 9) times more.
Next row (RS) (inc): P15 (17: 19), K2, P1, M1, moss st 5, M1, P1, K2, P15 (19: 19), K2, P1, M1, moss st 5, M1, P1, K2, P15 (17: 19). 71 (79: 83) sts.
Next row: K15 (17: 19), P2, K1, moss st 7, K1, P2, K15 (19: 19), P2, K1, moss st 7, K1, P2, K15 (17: 19).
Keeping patt correct as set, work a further 18 (20: 20) rows, ending with a WS row.

Next row (RS) (inc): P15 (17: 19), K2, P1, M1, moss st 7, M1, P1, K2, P15 (19: 19), K2, P1, M1, moss st 7, M1, P1, K2, P15 (17: 19). 75 (83: 87) sts.
Next row: K15 (17: 19), P2, K1, moss st 9, K1, P2, K15 (19: 19), P2, K1, moss st 9, K1, P2, K15 (17: 19).
Keeping patt correct as set, work a further 18 (20: 20) rows, ending with a WS row.
Next row (RS) (inc): P15 (17: 19), K2, P1, M1, moss st 9, M1, P1, K2, P15 (19: 19), K2, P1, M1, moss st 9, M1, P1, K2, P15 (17: 19). 79 (87: 91) sts.
Next row: K15 (17: 19), P2, K1, moss st 11, K1, P2, K15 (19: 19), P2, K1, moss st 11, K1, P2, K15 (17: 19).
Keeping patt correct, cont straight until back measures 26.5 (29: 30) cm, ending with a WS row.
Shape armholes
Keeping patt correct, cast off 3 (4: 4) sts at beg of next 2 rows. 73 (79: 83) sts.
Dec 1 st at each end of next 3 rows, then on foll 2 (3: 3) alt rows. 63 (67: 71) sts.
Work 5 rows, ending with a WS row.
Next row (RS): *P1, K1, rep from * to last st, P1.
Next row: as last row.
These 2 rows form moss st.
Keeping moss st correct, cont straight until armhole measures 19 (20.5: 21.5) cm, ending with a WS row.
Shape shoulders and back neck
Cast off 7 sts at beg of next 2 rows. 49 (53: 57) sts.
Next row (RS): Cast off 7 sts, patt until there are 10 (11: 12) sts on right needle and turn, leaving rem sts on a holder.
Work each side of neck separately.
Cast off 4 sts at beg of next row.
Cast off rem 6 (7: 8) sts.
With RS facing, rejoin yarn to rem sts, cast off centre 15 (17: 19) sts, patt to end.
Work to match first side, reversing shapings.

LEFT FRONT
Cast on 39 (43: 45) sts using 3¼mm (US 3) needles.
Work 7 rows in moss st as for back, ending with a RS row.
Next row (WS): Patt 6 sts and slip these sts onto a holder, patt to end. 33 (37: 39) sts.
Change to 4mm (US 6) needles.
Next row (RS): P15 (17: 19), K2, P1, moss st 5, P1, K2, P7 (9: 9).
Next row: K7 (9: 9), P2, K1, moss st 5, K1, P2, K15 (17: 19).
Rep last 2 rows 8 (8: 9) times more.
Next row (RS) (inc): P15 (17: 19), K2, P1, M1, moss st 5, M1, P1, K2, P7 (9: 9). 35 (39: 41) sts.
Next row: K7 (9: 9), P2, K1, moss st 7, K1, P2, K15 (17: 19).
Keeping patt correct as set, work a further 18 (20: 20) rows, ending with a WS row.
Next row (RS) (inc): P15 (17: 19), K2, P1, M1, moss st 7, M1, P1, K2, P7 (9: 9). 37 (41: 43) sts.
Next row: K7 (9: 9), P2, K1, moss st 9, K1, P2, K15 (17: 19).
Keeping patt correct as set, work a further 18 (20: 20) rows, ending with a WS row.
Next row (RS) (inc): P15 (17: 19), K2, P1, M1, moss st 9, M1, P1, K2, P7 (9: 9). 39 (43: 45) sts.
Next row: K7 (9: 9), P2, K1, moss st 11, K1, P2, K15 (17: 19).
Keeping patt correct, cont straight until left front matches back to beg of armhole shaping, ending with a WS row.
Shape armhole
Keeping patt correct, cast off 3 (4: 4) sts at beg of

next row. 36 (39: 41) sts.
Work 1 row.
Dec 1 st at armhole edge of next 3 rows, then on foll 2 (3: 3) alt rows. 31 (33: 35) sts.
Work 5 rows, ending with a WS row.
Keeping moss st correct as set by patt panels, cont in moss st over all sts, as folls:
Cont straight until 15 (15: 17) rows less have been worked than on back to start of shoulder shaping, ending with a RS row.
Shape neck
Cast off 6 (7: 7) sts at beg of next row. 25 (26: 28) sts.
Dec 1 st at neck edge of next 3 rows, then on foll 1 (1: 2) alt rows. 21 (22: 23) sts.
Work 3 rows.
Dec 1 st at neck edge of next row. 20 (21: 22) sts.
Work 5 rows, ending with a WS row.
Shape shoulder
Cast off 7 sts at beg of next and foll alt row.
Work 1 row. Cast off rem 6 (7: 8) sts.

RIGHT FRONT
Cast on 39 (43: 45) sts using 3¼mm (US 3) needles.
Work 4 rows in moss st as for back, ending with a WS row.
Next row (RS) (buttonhole row): Moss st 2, cast off 2 sts, moss st to end.
Next row: Moss st to end, casting on 2 sts over those cast off on previous row.
Work 1 row, ending with a RS row.
Next row (WS): Patt to last 6 sts and turn, leaving rem 6 sts on a holder. 33 (37: 39) sts.
Change to 4mm (US 6) needles.
Next row (RS): P7 (9: 9), K2, P1, moss st 5, P1, K2, P15 (17: 19).
Next row: K15 (17: 19), P2, K1, moss st 5, K1, P2, K7 (9: 9).
Rep last 2 rows 8 (8: 9) times more.
Next row (RS) (inc): P7 (9: 9), K2, P1, M1, moss st 5, M1, P1, K2, P15 (17: 19). 35 (39: 41) sts.
Next row: K15 (17: 19), P2, K1, moss st 7, K1, P2, K7 (9: 9).
Complete to match left front, reversing shapings.

LEFT SLEEVE
Sleeve front
Cast on 30 (30: 32) sts using 3¼mm (US 3) needles.
Row 1 (RS): *K1, P1, rep from * to end.
Row 2: *P1, K1, rep from * to end.
These 2 rows form moss st.
Keeping moss st correct, cont as folls:
Work a further 2 rows.
Next row (RS) (buttonhole row): Moss st 2, cast off 2 sts, moss st to end.
Next row: Moss st to end, casting on 2 sts over those cast off on previous row.
Work a further 2 rows in moss st.
Change to 4mm (US 6) needles.
Next row (RS): Moss st 5, K to last st, inc in last st. 31 (31: 33) sts.
Next row: P to last 5 sts, moss st 5.
Last 2 rows set st st with edge 5 sts still worked in moss st.
Keeping moss and st st correct as set, work a further 12 rows, inc 1 st at end of 7th (7th: 9th) row. 32 (32: 34) sts.
Break yarn and leave sts on a holder.
Sleeve back
Cast on 10 (12: 12) sts using 3¼mm (US 3) needles.
Row 1 (RS): *P1, K1, rep from * to end.
Row 2: *K1, P1, rep from * to end.
These 2 rows form moss st.
Keeping moss st correct, cont as folls:
Work a further 6 rows.
Change to 4mm (US 6) needles.

Next row (RS): Inc in first st, K to last 5 sts, moss st 5. 11 (13: 13) sts.
Next row: Moss st 5, P to end.
Last 2 rows set st st with edge 5 sts still worked in moss st.
Keeping moss and st st correct as set, work a further 12 rows, inc 1 st at beg of 7th (7th: 9th) row.
12 (14: 14) sts.

Join sections

Next row (RS): K across first 7 (9: 9) sts of sleeve back then, holding WS of sleeve front against RS of sleeve back, K tog first st of sleeve front with next st of sleeve back, K tog next 4 sts of sleeve front with rem 4 sts of sleeve back in same way, K rem 27 (27: 29) sts of sleeve front.
39 (41: 43) sts.
Beg with a P row, cont in st st, inc 1 st at each end of every foll 8th (8th: 10th) row from previous inc to 49 (59: 45) sts, then on every foll 6th (6th: 8th) row until there are 61 (63: 65) sts.
Cont straight until sleeve meas 36.5 (39.5: 42.5) cm from cast-on edge, ending with a WS row.

Shape top

Cast off 3 (4: 4) sts at beg of next 2 rows.
55 (55: 57) sts.
Dec 1 st at each end of next 3 rows, then on foll 2 alt rows. 45 (45: 47) sts.
Work 3 rows.
Dec 1 st at each end of next and every foll 4th row until 41 (37: 35) sts rem, then on every foll alt row until 29 (31: 33) sts rem.
Dec 1 st at each end of next 3 rows, ending with a WS row. 23 (25: 27) sts.
Cast off 4 sts at beg of next 2 rows.
Cast off rem 15 (17: 19) sts.

RIGHT SLEEVE

Sleeve back

Cast on 10 (12: 12) sts using 3¼mm (US 3) needles.
Row 1 (RS): *K1, P1, rep from * to end.
Row 2: *P1, K1, rep from * to end.
These 2 rows form moss st.
Keeping moss st correct, cont as folls:
Work a further 6 rows.
Change to 4mm (US 6) needles.
Next row (RS): Moss st 5, K to last st, inc in last st. 11 (13: 13) sts.
Next row: P to last 5 sts, moss st 5.
Last 2 rows set st st with edge 5 sts still worked in moss st.
Keeping moss and st st correct as set, work a further 12 rows, inc 1 st at end of 7th (7th: 9th) row.
12 (14: 14) sts.
Break yarn and leave sts on a holder.

Sleeve front

Cast on 30 (30: 32) sts using 3¼mm (US 3) needles.
Row 1 (RS): *P1, K1, rep from * to end.
Row 2: *K1, P1, rep from * to end.
These 2 rows form moss st.
Keeping moss st correct, cont as folls:
Work a further 2 rows.
Next row (RS) (buttonhole row): Moss st to last 4 sts, cast off 2 sts, moss st to end.
Next row: Moss st to end, casting on 2 sts over those cast off on previous row.
Work a further 2 rows in moss st.
Change to 4mm (US 6) needles.
Next row (RS): Inc in first st, K to last 5 sts, moss st 5. 31 (31: 33) sts.
Next row: Moss st 5, P to end.
Last 2 rows set st st with edge 5 sts still worked in moss st.
Keeping moss and st st correct as set, work a further 12 rows, inc 1 st at beg of 7th (7th: 9th) row. 32 (32: 34) sts.

Join sections

Next row (RS): K across first 27 (27: 29) sts of sleeve front, then holding WS of sleeve front against RS of sleeve back, K tog next st of sleeve front with first st of sleeve back, K tog rem 4 sts of sleeve front with next 4 sts of sleeve back in same way, K rem 7 (9: 9) sts of sleeve back.
39 (41: 43) sts.
Complete to match left sleeve.

MAKING UP

DO NOT PRESS.
Join shoulder seams using back stitch.

Button border

Slip 6 sts on left front holder onto 3¼mm (US 3) needles and rejoin yarn with RS facing.
Cont in moss st as set until border, when slightly stretched, fits up left front opening edge to neck, ending with a WS row.
Cast off. Slip stitch border in place.
Mark positions for 5 buttons on this border - lowest button level with buttonhole already worked in right front, top button 1.5 cm below neck shaping, and rem 3 buttons evenly spaced between.

Buttonhole border

Work to match button border, rejoining yarn with WS facing and with the addition of a further 4 buttonholes worked to correspond with positions marked for buttons as folls:
Buttonhole row (RS): Moss st 2, cast off 2 sts, moss st to end.
Next row: Moss st to end, casting on 2 sts over those cast-off on previous row.
Slip stitch border in place.

Collar

Cast on 75 (77: 79) sts using 3¼mm (US 3) needles.
Row 1 (RS): K3, P1, *K1, P1, rep from * to last 5 sts, K1, P1, K3.
Row 2: K1, P2, K1, moss st to last 4 sts, K1, P2, K1.
Row 3: K3, P1, M1, moss st to last 4 sts, M1, P1, K3.
Row 4: As row 2.
Row 5: K3, P1, moss st to last 4 sts, P1, K3.
Row 6: K1, P2, K1, M1, moss st to last 4 sts, M1, K1, P2, K1.
Row 7: As row 5.
Rep last 6 rows 3 times more and then row 2 again. 91 (93: 95) sts.
Cast off in patt.

Pocket flaps (make 2)

Cast on 21 sts using 3¼mm (US 3) needles.
Row 1 (RS): K3, P1, [K1, P1] 6 times, K1, P1, K3.
Row 2: K1, P2, K1, moss st 13, K1, P2, K1.
Row 3: K3, P1, moss st 13, P1, K3.
Rep last 2 rows 4 times more, and then row 2 again.

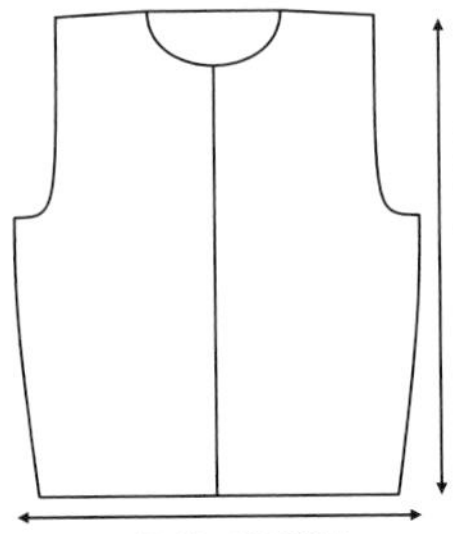
37 (41.5: 43) cm (14.5 (16.5: 17) in)
39.5 (43.5: 45.5) cm (15.5 (17: 18) in)

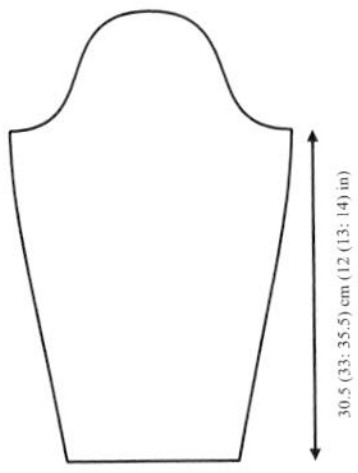
30.5 (33: 35.5) cm (12 (13: 14) in)

Row 13 (RS) (dec): K3, P1, work 2 tog, moss st to last 6 sts, work 2 tog tbl, P1, K3.
Row 14 (dec): K1, P2, K1, work 2 tog tbl, moss st to last 6 sts, work 2 tog, K1, P2, K1.
Rep rows 13 and 14 once more, and then row 13 again. 11 sts.
Row 18 (WS): K1, P2, K1, sl 1, K2tog, psso, K1, P2, K1.
Row 19: K3, sl 1, P2tog, psso, K3.
Row 20: K1, P1, sl 1, P2tog, psso, P1, K1.
Row 21: K1, sl 1, K2tog, psso, K1.
Row 22: Sl 1, K2tog, psso and fasten off.
Machine wash all pieces as described on the ball band before completing garment.
Placing centre of collar to centre back neck, sew cast on edge of collar evenly around neck edge, beg and ending halfway across front bands.
Sew pocket flaps in place at yoke over panels as in photograph - sew on flap using back stitch with flap pointing toward shoulder. Fold flap down and attach button through both layers.
See information page for finishing instructions, setting in sleeves using the set-in method.

Design number 6

Hero

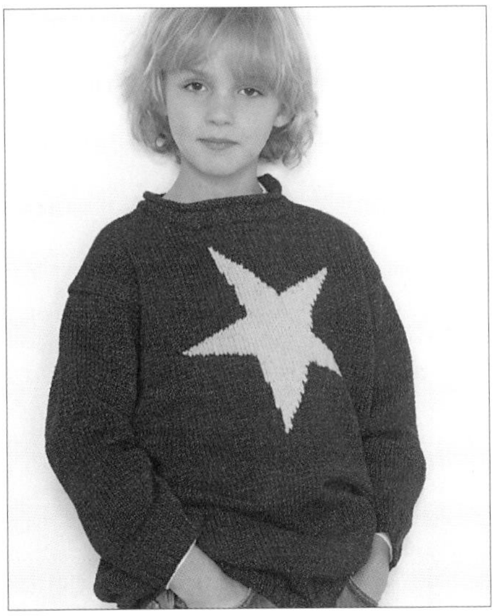

YARN

Rowan Denim

	4th	5th	6th	7th	8th	9th
To fit	2-3	3-4	4-5	6-7	8-9	9-10yrs
Chest size	22	23	24	26	28	30in
	56	58	61	66	71	76cm)
A Nash 225	7	8	10	11	13	15 x 50gm
B Ecru 324	1	1	1	1	1	1 x 50gm

NEEDLES

1 pair 3¾mm (no 9) (US 5) needles
1 pair 4mm (no 8) (US 6) needles

TENSION

Before washing 20 sts and 28 rows to 10 cm measured over stocking stitch using 4mm (US 6) needles.

Tension note: Denim will shrink in length when washed for the first time. Allowances have been made in this pattern for shrinkage (see size diagram for after washing measurements).

BACK

Cast on 75 (81: 87: 93: 101: 111) sts using 3¾mm (US 5) needles and yarn A.

Row 1 (RS): K0 (3: 0: 3: 1: 0), ★P3, K3, rep from ★ to last 3 (0: 3: 0: 4: 3) sts, P3 (0: 3: 0: 3: 3), K0 (0: 0: 0: 1: 0).

Row 2: P0 (3: 0: 3: 1: 0), ★K3, P3, rep from ★ to last 3 (0: 3: 0: 4: 3) sts, K3 (0: 3: 0: 3: 3), P0 (0: 0: 0: 1: 0).

Rep last 2 rows 3 times more.

Change to 4mm (US 6) needles and, beg with a K row, cont in st st as folls:

Cont straight until back measures 25.5 (30.5: 33.5: 36.5: 42.5: 45.5) cm, ending with a WS row.

Shape armholes

Cast off 5 (5: 5: 6: 6: 6) sts at beg of next 2 rows. 65 (71: 77: 81: 89: 99) sts.

Cont straight until armhole measures 20 (21: 23: 24: 26: 27.5) cm, ending with a WS row.

Shape shoulders and back neck

Cast off 6 (7: 8: 8: 9: 10) sts at beg of next 2 rows. 53 (57: 61: 65: 71: 79) sts.

Next row (RS): Cast off 6 (7: 8: 8: 9: 10) sts, K until there are 10 (11: 11: 12: 13: 15) sts on right needle and turn, leaving rem sts on a holder.

Work each side of neck separately.

Cast off 4 sts at beg of next row.

Cast off rem 6 (7: 7: 8: 9: 11) sts.

With RS facing, rejoin yarn to rem sts, cast off centre 21 (21: 23: 25: 27: 29) sts, K to end.

Work to match first side, reversing shapings.

FRONT

Cast on 75 (81: 87: 93: 101: 111) sts using 3¾mm (US 5) needles and yarn A.

Work 8 rows in rib as for back.

Change to 4mm (US 6) needles and, beg with a K row, cont in st st as folls:

Cont straight until front measures 15 (21: 25: 29: 36: 40) cm, ending with a WS row.

Join in yarn B and place motif as folls:

Next row (RS): K14 (17: 20: 23: 27: 32), starting with chart row 1 and using the INTARSIA method as described on the information page, work 47 sts from chart, K14 (17: 20: 23: 27: 32).

Next row: P14 (17: 20: 23: 27: 32), work across row 2 from chart, P14 (17: 20: 23: 27: 32).

Cont working from chart until chart row 73 has been completed and AT THE SAME TIME when front matches back to beg of armhole shaping, shape armholes as folls:

Shape armholes

Keeping chart correct, cast off 5 (5: 5: 6: 6: 6) sts at beg of next 2 rows. 65 (71: 77: 81: 89: 99) sts.

Cont straight until 12 (14: 14: 16: 16: 18) rows less have been worked than on back to start of shoulder shaping, ending with a WS row.

Shape neck

Next row (RS): K24 (28: 30: 32: 35: 40) and turn, leaving rem sts on a holder.

Work each side of neck separately.

Dec 1 st at neck edge of next 4 (4: 4: 6: 6: 6) rows, then on foll 1 (2: 2: 1: 1: 2) alt rows, and foll 4th row. 18 (21: 23: 24: 27: 31) sts.

Work 1 (1: 1: 3: 3: 3) rows.

Shape shoulder

Cast off 6 (7: 8: 8: 9: 10) sts at beg of next and foll alt row.

Work 1 row. Cast off rem 6 (7: 7: 8: 9: 11) sts.

With RS facing, rejoin yarn to rem sts, cast off centre 17 (15: 17: 17: 19: 19) sts, K to end.

Work to match first side, reversing shapings.

SLEEVES (both alike)

Cast on 39 (41: 43: 47: 49: 51) sts using 3¾mm (US 5) needles and yarn A.

Row 1 (RS): P0 (0: 0: 1: 2: 0), K0 (1: 2: 3: 3: 0), ★P3, K3, rep from ★ to last 3 (4: 5: 1: 2: 3) sts, P3 (3: 3: 1: 2: 3), K0 (1: 2: 0: 0: 0).

Row 2: K0 (0: 0: 1: 2: 0), P0 (1: 2: 3: 3: 0), ★K3, P3, rep from ★ to last 3 (4: 5: 1: 2: 3) sts, K3 (3: 3: 1: 2: 3), P0 (1: 2: 0: 0: 0).

Rep last 2 rows 3 times more.

Change to 4mm (US 6) needles and, beg with a K row, cont in st st, inc 1 st at each end of next and every foll 6th row to 45 (47: 51: 69: 73: 75) sts, then on every foll 4th row until there are 67 (71: 77: 81: 87: 93) sts.

Cont straight until sleeve measures 29 (30.5: 34: 40: 43: 46) cm, ending with a WS row.

Cast off loosely.

MAKING UP
DO NOT PRESS.

Join right shoulder seam using back stitch.

Neck border

With RS facing, using yarn A and 3¾mm (US 5) needles, pick up and knit 13 (14: 15: 15: 15: 17) sts down left front neck, 17 (15: 17: 17: 19: 19) sts across front neck, 13 (14: 15: 15: 15: 17) sts up right front neck, and 29 (29: 31: 31: 35: 37) sts across back neck.

72 (72: 78: 78: 84: 90) sts.

Row 1 (WS): ★K3, P3, rep from ★ to end.

Rep last row 6 times more, ending with a WS row.

Beg with a K row, work 8 rows in st st.

Cast off loosely knitwise.

Join left shoulder and neck border seam using back stitch, reversing seam for st st roll.

Machine wash all pieces as described on the ball band before completing garment.

Set sleeves into armholes using the square set-in method described on the information page.

See information page for finishing instructions.

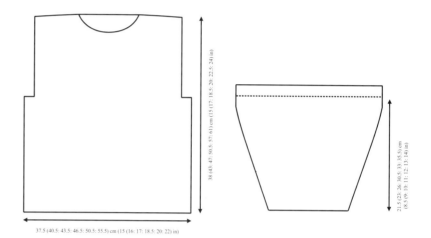

37.5 (40.5: 43.5: 46.5: 50.5: 55.5) cm (15 (16: 17: 18.5: 20: 22) in)

Key □ A ● B

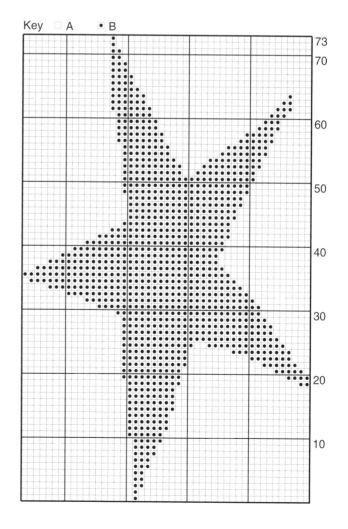

Billie

YARN

Rowan Wool Cotton

	4th	5th	6th	7th	8th	9th
To fit						
	2-3	3-4	4-5	6-7	8-9	9-10 yrs
Chest size						
	22	23	24	26	28	30 in
	(56	58	61	66	71	76 cm)
	3	3	4	4	5	5 x 50gm

(crew neck version photographed in Riviera 930, V neck version in Inky 908)

NEEDLES

1 pair 3¾mm (no 9) (US 5) needles
1 pair 4mm (no 8) (US 6) needles

TENSION

22 sts and 30 rows to 10 cm measured over stocking stitch using 4mm (US 6) needles.

BACK

Cast on 63 (67: 73: 79: 87: 95) sts using 3¾mm (US 5) needles.
Row 1 (RS): P0 (0: 2: 0: 0: 1), K0 (2: 3: 2: 0: 3), *P3, K3, rep from * to last 3 (5: 2: 5: 3: 1) sts, P3 (3: 2: 3: 3: 1), K0 (2: 0: 2: 0: 0).
Row 2: K0 (0: 2: 0: 0: 1), P0 (2: 3: 2: 0: 3), *K3,

P3, rep from * to last 3 (5: 2: 5: 3: 1) sts, K3 (3: 2: 3: 3: 1), P0 (2: 0: 2: 0: 0).
Last 2 rows form rib.
Work a further 8 (8: 10: 10: 12: 14) rows in rib.
Change to 4mm (US 6) needles and, beg with a K row, cont in st st as folls:
Work straight until back measures 21 (22: 24.5: 26: 28.5: 30) cm, ending with a WS row.
Shape armholes
Cast off 3 (3: 4: 4: 4: 4) sts at beg of next 2 rows. 57 (61: 65: 71: 79: 87) sts.
Dec 1 st at both ends of next 3 (3: 3: 3: 5: 5) rows, then on every foll alt row until 49 (53: 55: 61: 65: 73) sts rem.
Cont straight until armhole measures 13 (14: 15: 16: 17: 18) cm, ending with a WS row.
Shape shoulders and back neck
Cast off 4 (4: 5: 5: 6: 7) sts at beg of next 2 rows. 41 (45: 45: 51: 53: 59) sts.
Next row (RS): Cast off 4 (4: 5: 5: 6: 7) sts, K until there are 8 (9: 8: 10: 9: 10) sts on right needle and turn, leaving rem sts on a holder.
Work each side of neck separately.
Cast off 4 sts at beg of next row.
Cast off rem 4 (5: 4: 6: 5: 6) sts.
With RS facing, rejoin yarn to rem sts, cast off centre 17 (19: 19: 21: 23: 25) sts, K to end.
Work to match first side, reversing shapings.

CREW NECK VERSION FRONT

Work as for back until 12 (12: 14: 14: 16: 16) rows less have been worked than on back to start of shoulder shaping, ending with a WS row.
Shape neck
Next row (RS): K18 (19: 21: 23: 25: 28) and turn, leaving rem sts on a holder.
Work each side of neck separately.
Dec 1 st at neck edge of next 4 rows, then on every foll alt row until 12 (13: 14: 16: 17: 20) sts rem.
Work 3 rows.
Shape shoulder
Cast off 4 (4: 5: 5: 6: 7) sts at beg of next and foll alt row.
Work 1 row.
Cast off rem 4 (5: 4: 6: 5: 6) sts.
With RS facing, rejoin yarn to rem sts, cast off centre 13 (15: 13: 15: 15: 17) sts, K to end.
Work to match first side, reversing shapings.

V NECK VERSION FRONT

Work as for back until 22 (24: 28: 30: 34: 36) rows less have been worked than on back to start of shoulder shaping, ending with a WS row.
Shape neck
Next row (RS): K24 (26: 27: 30: 32: 36) and turn, leaving rem sts on a holder.
Work each side of neck separately.
4th, 5th, 6th and 7th sizes only
Dec 1 st at neck edge of next 6 (6: 2: 2) rows. 18 (20: 25: 28) sts.
All sizes
Work 1 row.
Dec 1 st at neck edge of next and every foll alt row until 12 (13: 14: 16: 17: 20) sts rem.
Work 3 rows.
Shape shoulder
Cast off 4 (4: 5: 5: 6: 7) sts at beg of next and foll alt row.
Work 1 row.
Cast off rem 4 (5: 4: 6: 5: 6) sts.
With RS facing, rejoin yarn to rem sts, K2tog, K to end.
Work to match first side, reversing shapings.

MAKING UP

PRESS all pieces as described on the information page.
Join right shoulder seam using back stitch.
Crew neck border
With RS facing and 3¾mm (US 5) needles, pick up and knit 13 (12: 16: 15: 15: 17) sts down left front neck, 13 (15: 13: 15: 15: 17) sts across front neck, 13 (12: 16: 15: 15: 17) sts up right front neck, and 27 (27: 27: 27: 33: 33) sts across back neck. 66 (66: 72: 72: 78: 84) sts.
Row 1 (WS): *K3, P3, rep from * to end.
Rep last row 4 times more, ending with a WS row.
Cast off evenly in rib.

V neck border
With RS facing and 3¾mm (US 5) needles, pick up and knit 21 (21: 27: 27: 33: 33) sts down left front neck, place marker on needle, 21 (21: 27: 27: 33: 33) sts up right front neck, and 27 (27: 27: 27: 33: 33) sts across back neck. 69 (69: 81: 81: 99: 99) sts.
Row 1 (WS): [K3, P3] 8 (8: 9: 9: 11: 11) times, slip marker to right needle, [P3, K3] 3 (3: 4: 4: 5: 5) times, P3.
This row sets position of rib.
Keeping rib correct, cont as folls:
Row 2 (RS): Rib to within 2 sts of marker, K2tog tbl, slip marker to right needle, K2tog, rib to end.
Row 3: Rib to within 2 sts of marker, P2tog, slip marker to right needle, P2tog tbl, rib to end.
Rep last 2 rows once more, ending with a WS row.
Cast off evenly in rib, decreasing 1 st either side of marker as before.

Crew and V neck versions
Join left shoulder and neck border seam using back stitch.
Armhole borders
With RS facing and 3¾mm (US 5) needles, pick up and knit 60 (66: 72: 78: 84: 90) sts around armhole edge.
Row 1 (WS): *K3, P3, rep from * to end.
Rep last row 3 times more, ending with a RS row.
Cast off evenly in rib.
See information page for finishing instructions.

28.5 (30.5: 33: 36: 39.5: 43) cm
(11 (12: 13: 14: 15.5: 17) in)

34 (36: 39.5: 42: 45.5: 48) cm
(13.5 (14: 15.5: 16.5: 18: 19) in)

Crumpet

YARN

Rowan Chunky Tweed

	5th	6th	7th	8th	9th	
To fit	3-4	4-5	6-7	8-9	9-10	yrs
Chest size	23	24	26	28	30	in
	(58	61	66	71	76	cm)
	8	9	11	12	14	x 100gm

(photographed in Polar 879)

NEEDLES

1 pair 6mm (no 4) (US 10) needles
1 pair 6½mm (no 3) (US 10½) needles

BUTTONS - 6

TENSION

13 sts and 22 rows to 10 cm measured over moss stitch using 6½mm (US 10½) needles.

BACK

Cast on 61 (65: 71: 77: 83) sts using 6mm (US 10) needles.
1st row (RS): K1, *P1, K1, rep from * to end.
2nd row: As 1st row.
These 2 rows form moss st.
Cont in moss for a further 8 rows.
Change to 6½mm (US 10½) needles and cont in moss st until back measures 31.5 (35: 37: 43: 45.5) cm from cast-on edge, ending with a WS row.
Shape armholes
Keeping patt correct, cast off 4 sts at beg of next 2 rows.
53 (57: 63: 69: 75) sts.
Cont straight until armhole measures 19.5 (21: 22.5: 24: 25.5) cm, ending with a WS row.
Shape shoulders and back neck
Cast off 6 (6: 7: 8: 8) sts at beg of next 2 rows.
41 (45: 49: 53: 59) sts.
Next row (RS): Cast off 6 (6: 7: 8: 8) sts, patt until there are 9 (10: 11: 11: 13) sts on right needle and turn, leaving rem sts on a holder.
Work each side of neck separately.
Cast off 4 sts at beg of next row.
Cast off rem 5 (6: 7: 7: 9) sts.
With RS facing, rejoin yarn to rem sts, cast off centre 11 (13: 13: 15: 17) sts, patt to end.
Work to match first side, reversing shapings.

POCKET LININGS (make 2)

Cast on 15 (17: 17: 19: 19) sts using 6½mm (US 10½) needles.
Work 12 (13: 14: 15: 16) cm in moss st as given for back, ending with a RS row.
Break yarn and leave sts on a holder.

LEFT FRONT

Cast on 35 (37: 41: 43: 47) sts using 6mm (US 10) needles.
Work 10 rows in moss st as given for back.
Change to 6½mm (US 10½) needles and cont in moss st until left front measures 19 (20: 22: 24: 26) cm from cast-on edge, ending with a WS row.
Place pocket
Next row (RS): Moss st 4 (4: 6: 6: 8), cast off next 15 (17: 17: 19: 19) sts in moss st, moss st to end.
Next row: Moss st 16 (16: 18: 18: 20), with WS facing moss st across 15 (17: 17: 19: 19) sts of first pocket lining, moss st rem 4 (4: 6: 6: 8) sts of front.
Cont straight until left front matches back to beg of armhole shaping, ending with a WS row.
Shape armhole
Keeping patt correct, cast off 4 sts at beg of next row.
31 (33: 37: 39: 43) sts.
Cont straight until left front matches back to start of shoulder shaping, ending with a WS row.
Shape shoulder
Cast off 6 (6: 7: 8: 8) sts at beg of next and foll alt row, then 5 (6: 7: 7: 9) sts at beg of foll alt row.
Work 1 row on rem 14 (15: 16: 16: 18) sts.
Break yarn and leave sts on a holder.
Mark positions for 6 buttons on this front - first button to be 6cm below pocket opening, last button to be 3.5cm below start of shoulder shaping and rem 4 buttons evenly spaced between.

RIGHT FRONT

Cast on 35 (37: 41: 43: 47) sts using 6mm (US 10) needles.
Work 10 rows in moss st as given for back.
Change to 6½mm (US 10½) needles and cont in moss st until right front measures 13 (14: 16: 18: 20) cm from cast-on edge, ending with a WS row.
Next row (RS) (buttonhole row): Moss st 4, cast off 2 sts, moss st to end.
Next row: Moss st to end, casting on 2 sts over those cast off on previous row.
Cont straight until right front measures 19 (20: 22: 24: 26) cm from cast-on edge, ending with a WS row.
Place pocket
Next row (RS): Moss st 16 (16: 18: 18: 20), cast off next 15 (17: 17: 19: 19) sts in moss st, moss st to end.
Next row: Moss st 4 (4: 6: 6: 8), with WS facing moss st across 15 (17: 17: 19: 19) sts of second pocket lining, moss st rem 16 (16: 18: 18: 20) sts of front.
Cont straight until right front matches back to beg of armhole shaping, ending with a RS row.
Shape armhole
Keeping patt correct, cast off 4 sts at beg of next row. 31 (33: 37: 39: 43) sts.
Cont straight until right front matches back to start of shoulder shaping, ending with a RS row.
Shape shoulder
Cast off 6 (6: 7: 8: 8) sts at beg of next and foll alt row, then 5 (6: 7: 7: 9) sts at beg of foll alt row.
Do NOT break yarn.
Leave rem 14 (15: 16: 16: 18) sts on a holder and set aside ball of yarn - this will be used for hood.

SLEEVES (both alike)

Cast on 35 (37: 39: 41: 43) sts using 6mm (US 10) needles.
Work 20 rows in moss st as given for back.
Change to 6½mm (US 10½) needles.
Cont in moss st, inc 1 st at each end of 3rd and every foll 3rd (3rd: 4th: 4th: 4th) row until there are 51 (55: 59: 63: 67) sts.
Cont straight until sleeve measures 26 (29: 33.5: 36: 38.5) cm, ending with a WS row.
Cast off loosely.

MAKING UP

PRESS all pieces as described on the info page. Join shoulder seams using back stitch.
Hood
With RS facing, using ball of yarn left at right front neck edge and 6½mm (US 10½) needles, patt across 14 (15: 16: 16: 18) sts of right front, pick up and knit 19 (21: 21: 23: 25) sts across back neck, placing marker on centre st, then patt across 14 (15: 16: 16: 18) sts of left front.
47 (51: 53: 55: 61) sts.
Keeping moss st correct as set, cont as folls:
Work 3 rows.
Next row (RS) (inc): Moss st to marked st, M1, moss st 1, M1, moss st to end.
Rep last 4 rows 3 times more.
55 (59: 61: 63: 69) sts.
Cont straight until hood measures 26 (27: 28: 29: 30) cm, ending with a WS row.
Next row (RS) (dec): Moss st to within 2 sts of marked st, work 2 tog tbl, k1, work 2 tog, moss st to end.
Work 1 row.
Rep last 2 rows twice more, dec 1 st at centre of last row. 48 (52: 54: 56: 62) sts.
Next row (RS): Moss st 24 (26: 27: 28: 31) and turn.
Fold hood in half with WS facing and, using a spare needle, cast off sts from each needle tog to form hood seam.
Pocket flaps (make 2)
Cast on 17 (19: 19: 21: 21) sts using 6½mm (US 10½) needles.
Work 8 (10: 10: 12: 12) rows in moss st as given for back.
Cast off.
Sew pocket flaps to fronts just above pocket openings, using photograph as a guide.
See information page for finishing instructions, setting in sleeves using the square set-in method.

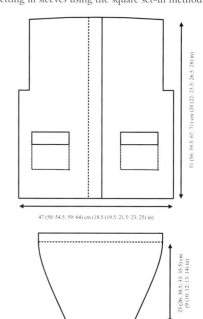

51 (56: 59.5: 67: 71) cm (20 (22: 23.5: 26.5: 28) in)

47 (50: 54.5: 59: 64) cm (18.5 (19.5: 21.5: 23: 25) in)

23 (26: 30.5: 33: 35.5) cm (9 (10: 12: 13: 14) in)

Muffin

YARN

Rowan DK Soft

	5th	6th	7th	8th	9th	
To fit	3-4	4-5	6-7	8-9	9-10	yrs
Chest size	23	24	26	28	30in	
	(58	61	66	71	76cm)	
A Tawny	171 3	4	4	5	5 x 50gm	
B Luna	173 2	2	3	3	3 x 50gm	

NEEDLES

1 pair 3¼mm (no 10) (US 3) needles
1 pair 4mm (no 8) (US 6) needles

BUTTONS - 5

TENSION

23 sts and 32 rows to 10 cm measured over
patterned stocking stitch using 4mm (US 6) needles.

LEFT FRONT

Note: The front band is knitted at the same time
as the left front. The slipped st marks the front
opening edge and the 7 sts beyond this will be
turned to the WS to form a facing and slip
stitched into position.
Cast on 48 (51: 55: 60: 63) sts using 3¼mm (US 3)
needles and yarn A.
Row 1 (RS): K to last 8 sts, with yarn at back
of work slip next st purlwise, K7.
Row 2: P8, K to end.
Rep last 2 rows twice more.
Change to 4mm (US 6) needles.
Work in patt from front chart as folls:
Cont in patt until chart row 60 (66: 70: 78: 80)
has been completed, ending with a WS row.
Shape armhole
Keeping chart correct, cast off 3 sts at beg of
next row. 45 (48: 52: 57: 60) sts.
Work 1 row.
Dec 1 st at armhole edge of next 3 (3: 4: 4: 4) rows.
42 (45: 48: 53: 56) sts.
Cont straight until chart row 99 (107: 113: 121: 125)
has been completed, ending with a RS row.
Shape neck
Keeping chart correct, cast off 15 (15: 15: 15: 16) sts
at beg of next row. 27 (30: 33: 38: 40) sts.
Dec 1 st at neck edge of next 5 rows, then on
every foll alt row until 19 (22: 24: 28: 29) sts rem.

Work 1 row, ending with chart row
112 (120: 128: 138: 144).
Shape shoulder
Cast off 6 (7: 8: 9: 10) sts at beg of next and foll
alt row.
Work 1 row. Cast off rem 7 (8: 8: 10: 9) sts.

RIGHT FRONT

Cast on 48 (51: 55: 60: 63) sts using 3¼mm (US 3)
needles and yarn A.
Row 1 (RS): K7, with yarn at back of work
slip next st purlwise, K to end.
Row 2: K to last 8 sts, P8.
Rep last 2 rows twice more.
Change to 4mm (US 6) needles.
Work in patt from front chart as folls:
Work 16 (16: 14: 14: 18) rows.
Buttonhole row (RS): Keeping colour patt
correct as set on chart, K2, K2tog, yfwd, K3,
with yarn at back of work slip next st purlwise,

K3, yfwd, K2tog tbl, K to end.
Working a further 4 buttonholes on every foll
20th (22nd: 24th: 26th: 26th) row as set by last
row, cont in patt from chart and complete to
match left front, reversing all shapings.

SLEEVES (both alike)

Cast on 42 (42: 46: 48: 48) sts using 3¼mm (US 3)
needles and yarn A.
Knit 6 rows.
Change to 4mm (US 6) needles.
Work in patt from back and sleeve chart, inc 1 st
at each end of 5th and every foll 4th row until there
are 76 (76: 74: 76: 76) sts, taking inc sts into patt.
6th, 7th, 8th and 9th sizes only
Inc 1 st at each end of every foll 6th row until
there are – (80: 84: 88: 92) sts.
All sizes
Cont straight until chart row 78 (88: 102: 112: 124)
has been completed, ending with a WS row.

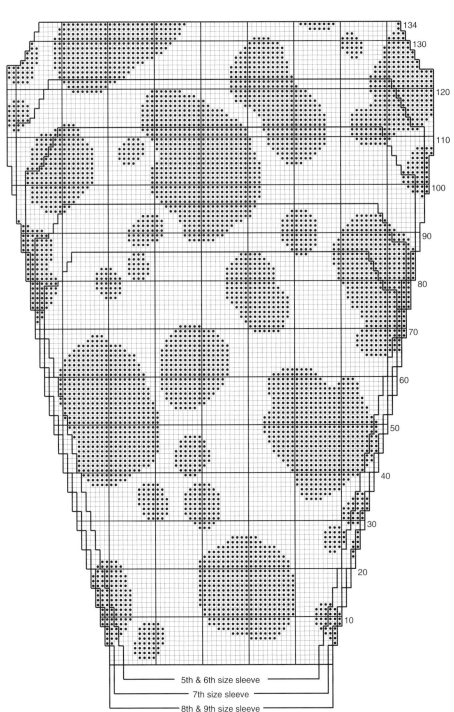

5th & 6th size sleeve
7th size sleeve
8th & 9th size sleeve

Shape top
Keeping chart correct, cast off 3 sts at beg of next 2 rows.
70 (74: 78: 82: 86) sts.
Dec 1 st at each end of next and foll 2 (2: 3: 3: 3) alt rows.
Work 1 row.
Cast off rem 64 (68: 70: 74: 78) sts.

BACK
Cast on 75 (81: 89: 99: 105) sts using 3¼mm (US 3) needles and yarn A.
Knit 6 rows.
Change to 4mm (US 6) needles.
Using the **intarsia** technique described on the information page, starting and ending rows as indicated, and beg with a K row, work in patt

from back and sleeves chart, which is worked entirely in st st, as folls:
Cont in patt until chart row 60 (66: 70: 78: 80) has been completed, ending with a WS row.
Shape armholes
Keeping chart correct, cast off 3 sts at beg of next 2 rows.
69 (75: 83: 93: 99) sts.

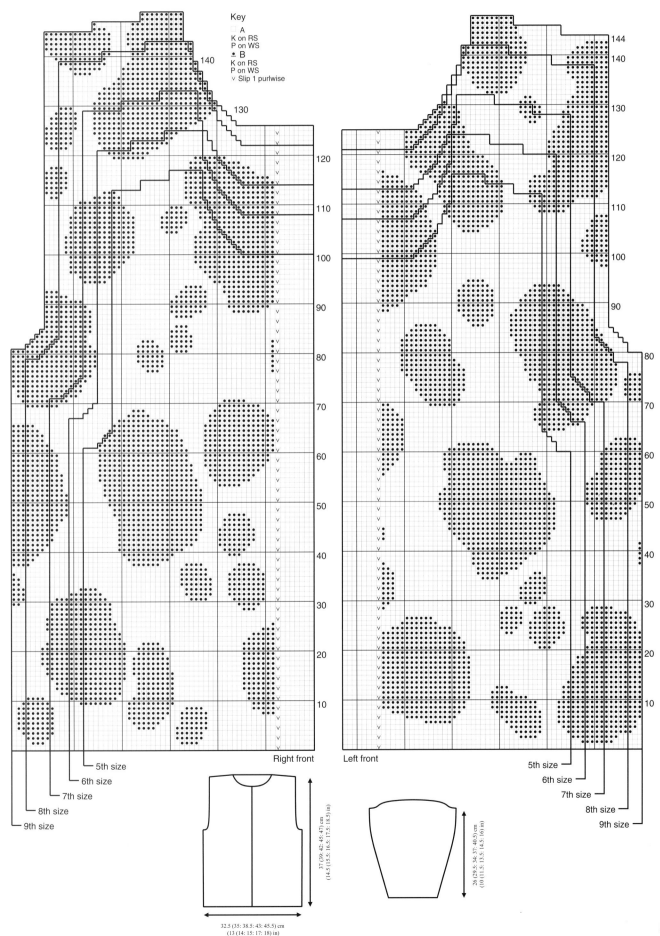

Key
A
K on RS
P on WS
• B
K on RS
P on WS
v Slip 1 purlwise

Right front

Left front

5th size
6th size
7th size
8th size
9th size

5th size
6th size
7th size
8th size
9th size

37 (39: 42: 45: 47) cm
(14.5 (15.5: 16.5: 17.5: 18.5) in)

32.5 (35: 38.5: 43: 45.5) cm
(13 (14: 15: 17: 18) in)

26 (29.5: 34: 37: 40.5) cm
(10 (11.5: 13.5: 14.5: 16) in)

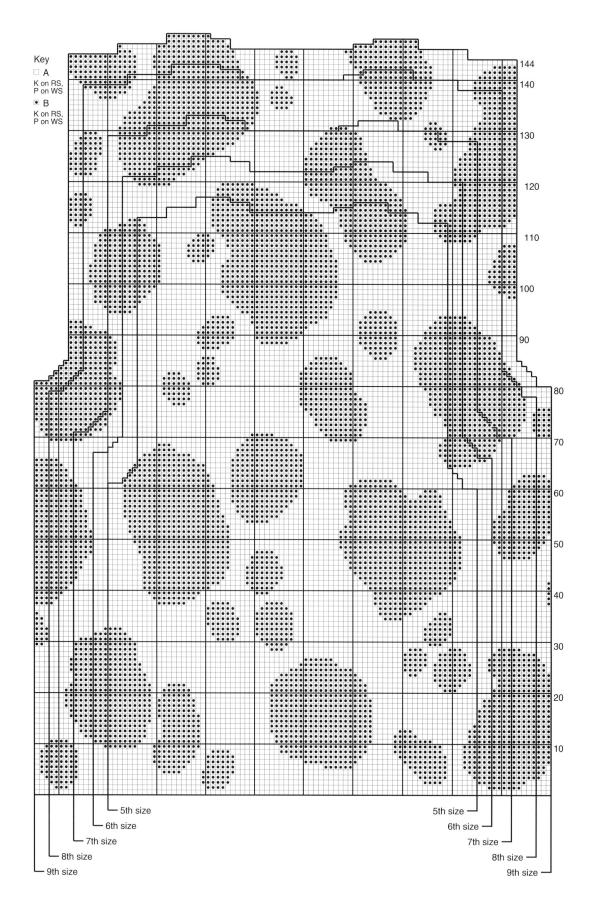

Key

□ A
K on RS,
P on WS

● B
K on RS,
P on WS

144
140
130
120
110
100
90
80
70
60
50
40
30
20
10

5th size
6th size
7th size
8th size
9th size

5th size
6th size
7th size
8th size
9th size

Dec 1 st at each end of next 3 (3: 4: 4: 4) rows.
63 (69: 75: 85: 91) sts.Cont straight until chart
row 112 (120: 128: 138: 144) has been
completed, ending with a WS row.

Shape shoulders and back neck

Cast off 6 (7: 8: 9: 10) sts at beg of next 2 rows.
51 (55: 59: 67: 71) sts.

Next row (RS): Cast off 6 (7: 8: 9: 10) sts, patt
until there are 11 (12: 12: 14: 13) sts on right
needle and turn, leaving rem sts on a holder.
Work each side of neck separately.

Cast off 4 sts at beg of next row.
Cast off rem 7 (8: 8: 10: 9) sts.
With RS facing, rejoin yarn to rem sts, cast off
centre 17 (17: 19: 21: 25) sts, patt to end.
Work to match first side, reversing shapings.

COLLAR

Cast on 67 (67: 75: 83: 91) sts using 3¼mm (US 3)
needles and yarn A.
Work in garter st for 7 (7: 8: 8: 8) cm.
Cast off knitwise.

MAKING UP

PRESS all pieces as described on the
information page.
Join shoulder seams using back stitch. Fold front
opening edges to inside along slipped stitch line
and carefully slip stitch into position. Neatly
oversew around buttonholes. Positioning ends of
collar 4 sts in from front opening edges, stitch
cast-off edge of collar to neck edge.
See info page for finishing instructions, setting in
sleeves using the shallow set-in sleeve method.

Jolly

YARN
Rowan 4-ply Botany

	4th	5th	6th	7th	8th	9th	
To fit	2-3	3-4	4-5	6-7	8-9	9-10	yrs
Chest size	22	23	24	26	28	30	in
	(56	58	61	66	71	76	cm)
A Redwd 549	1	1	1	1	1	2	x50gm
B Lavender 571	2	2	2	3	3	3	x50gm
C Frsh Grn 573	1	2	2	2	2	2	x50gm
D Frost 552	1	1	1	1	1	1	x50gm
E Lilac Ice 570	1	2	2	2	2	2	x50gm

NEEDLES
1 pair 2¾mm (no 12) (US 2) needles
1 pair 3¼mm (no 10) (US 3) needles

BUTTONS - 7

TENSION
28 sts and 36 rows to 10 cm measured over plain stocking stitch using 3¼mm (US 3) needles.
30 sts and 34 rows to 10 cm measured over patterned stocking stitch using 3¼mm (US 3) needles.

BACK
Cast on 153 (171: 183: 201: 225: 237) sts using 2¾mm (US 2) needles and yarn B.
Row 1 (RS): K3, *cast off 3 sts, K3, rep from * to end. 78 (87: 93: 102: 114: 120) sts.
Knit 1 row, inc 1 st at centre for 4th size and dec

1 st at centre for 7th, 8th and 9th sizes. 79 (87: 93: 101: 113: 119) sts.
Break off yarn B and join in yarn C.
Knit 2 rows.
Change to 3¼mm (US 3) needles and, beg with a K row, cont in st st as folls:
Inc 1 st at each end of 9th (11th: 11th: 11th: 13th: 13th) and every foll 10th (10th: 12th: 10th: 12th: 12th) row until there are 85 (93: 99: 109: 121: 127) sts.
Cont straight until back measures 12.5 (13: 14.5: 16: 18: 19) cm from lower edge, ending with a RS row.
Next row (inc) (WS): P7 (6: 7: 5: 7: 4), *inc in next st, P13 (15: 11: 13: 14: 12), rep from * to last 8 (7: 8: 6: 9: 6) sts, inc in next st, P7 (6: 7: 5: 8: 5). 91 (99: 107: 117: 129: 137) sts.
Using the **fairisle** technique described on the information page, starting and ending rows as indicated, working rows 1 to 10 once only and then repeating rows 11 to 26 as required, and beg with a K row, work in patt from chart, which is worked entirely in st st, as folls:
Cont in patt until chart row 14 is completed, ending with a WS row.
Shape armholes
Keeping chart correct, cast off 3 (3: 3: 4: 4: 4) sts at beg of next 2 rows. 85 (93: 101: 109: 121: 129) sts.
Dec 1 st at each end of next 5 rows, then on every foll alt row until 69 (77: 85: 91: 103: 111) sts rem.
Cont straight until armhole measures 15 (16: 17: 18: 19: 20) cm, ending with a WS row.
Shape shoulders and back neck
Cast off 6 (7: 8: 9: 11: 12) sts at beg of next 2 rows. 57 (63: 69: 73: 81: 87) sts.
Next row (RS): Cast off 6 (7: 8: 9: 11: 12) sts, patt until there are 11 (12: 13: 13: 14: 15) sts on right needle and turn, leaving rem sts on a holder.
Work each side of neck separately.
Cast off 4 sts at beg of next row.
Cast off rem 7 (8: 9: 9: 10: 11) sts.
With RS facing, rejoin yarn to rem sts, cast off centre 23 (25: 27: 29: 31: 33) sts, patt to end.
Work to match first side, reversing shapings.

LEFT FRONT
Cast on 75 (87: 93: 99: 111: 117) sts using 2¾mm (US 2) needles and yarn B.
Row 1 (RS): K3, *cast off 3 sts, K3, rep from * to end. 39 (45: 48: 51: 57: 60) sts.
Knit 1 row, inc 1 st at centre for 4th size and dec 1 st at centre for 5th and 6th sizes.
40 (44: 47: 51: 57: 60) sts.
Break off yarn B and join in yarn C.
Knit 2 rows.
Change to 3¼mm (US 3) needles and, beg with a K row, cont in st st as folls:
Inc 1 st at beg of 9th (11th: 11th: 11th: 13th: 13th)

and every foll 10th (10th: 12th: 10th: 12th: 12th) row until there are 43 (47: 50: 55: 61: 64) sts.
Cont straight until left front measures 12.5 (13: 14.5: 16: 18: 19) cm from lower edge, ending with a RS row.
Next row (inc) (WS): P7 (7: 5: 6: 7: 5), *inc in next st, P13 (15: 12: 13: 14: 12), rep from * to last 8 (8: 6: 7: 9: 7) sts, inc in next st, P7 (7: 5: 6: 8: 6). 46 (50: 54: 59: 65: 69) sts.
Work in patt from chart as folls:
Cont straight until chart row 14 is completed, ending with a WS row.
Shape armhole
Keeping chart correct, cast off 3 (3: 3: 4: 4: 4) sts at beg of next row. 43 (47: 51: 55: 61: 65) sts.
Work 1 row.
Dec 1 st at armhole edge of next 5 rows, then on every foll alt row until 35 (39: 43: 46: 52: 56) sts rem.
Cont straight until 11 (13: 13: 15: 17: 19) rows less have been worked than on back to start of shoulder shaping, ending with a RS row.
Shape neck
Keeping patt correct, cast off 10 (10: 11: 11: 11: 11) sts at beg of next row. 25 (29: 32: 35: 41: 45) sts.
Dec 1 st at neck edge of next 5 rows, then on every foll alt row until 19 (22: 25: 27: 32: 35) sts rem.
Work 3 rows, ending with a WS row.
Shape shoulder
Cast off 6 (7: 8: 9: 11: 12) sts at beg of next and foll alt row.
Work 1 row. Cast off rem 7 (8: 9: 9: 10: 11) sts.

RIGHT FRONT
Cast on 75 (87: 93: 99: 111: 117) sts using 2¾mm (US 2) needles and yarn B.
Row 1 (RS): K3, *cast off 3 sts, K3, rep from * to end. 39 (45: 48: 51: 57: 60) sts.
Knit 1 row, inc 1 st at centre for 4th size and dec 1 st at centre for 5th and 6th sizes.
40 (44: 47: 51: 57: 60) sts.
Break off yarn B and join in yarn C.
Knit 2 rows.
Change to 3¼mm (US 3) needles and, beg with a K row, cont in st st as folls:
Inc 1 st at end of 9th (11th: 11th: 11th: 13th: 13th) and every foll 10th (10th: 12th: 10th: 12th: 12th) row until there are 43 (47: 50: 55: 61: 64) sts.
Complete to match left front, reversing shapings.

SLEEVES (both alike)
Cast on 161 (169: 177: 185: 193: 201) sts using 2¾mm (US 2) needles and yarn A.
Break off yarn A and join in yarn B.
Row 1 (RS): K1, *K2, lift first of these 2 sts over 2nd st and off right needle, rep from * to end. 81 (85: 89: 93: 97: 101) sts.
Row 2: P1, *P2tog, rep from * to end. 41 (43: 45: 47: 49: 51) sts.

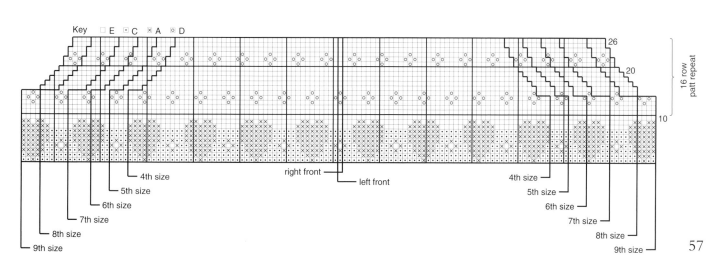

Key □ E · C × A ○ D

right front
left front

4th size
5th size
6th size
7th size
8th size
9th size

4th size
5th size
6th size
7th size
8th size
9th size

10
20
26
16 row patt repeat

Row 3: P0 (0: 1: 0: 0: 0), K2 (3: 3: 0: 1: 2), ★P2, K3, rep from ★ to last 4 (0: 1: 2: 3: 4) sts, P2 (0: 1: 2: 2: 2), K2 (0: 0: 0: 1: 2).

Row 4: K0 (0: 1: 0: 0: 0), P2 (3: 3: 0: 1: 2), ★K2, P3, rep from ★ to last 4 (0: 1: 2: 3: 4) sts, K2 (0: 1: 2: 2: 2), P2 (0: 0: 0: 1: 2).

Rows 3 and 4 form rib.

Work a further 2 rows in rib.

Change to 3¼mm (US 3) needles.

Cont in rib as set, inc 1 st at each end of next and every foll 6th row to 51 (55: 63: 75: 81: 85) sts, then on every foll 4th row until there are 75 (81: 85: 89: 95: 101) sts, taking inc sts into rib.

Cont straight until sleeve measures 24 (26.5: 29.5: 33.5: 37: 40.5) cm from beg of rib, ending with a WS row.

Shape top

Keeping rib correct, cast off 3 (3: 3: 4: 4: 4) sts at beg of next 2 rows. 69 (75: 79: 81: 87: 93) sts.

Dec 1 st at each end of next and foll 4 (4: 4: 5: 5: 5) alt rows.

Work 1 row. Cast off rem 59 (65: 69: 69: 75: 81) sts.

MAKING UP

PRESS all pieces as described on the info page. Join shoulder seams using back stitch.

Button border

With RS facing, yarn D and 2¾mm (US 2) needles, pick up and knit 75 (81: 87: 93: 99: 105) sts along left front opening edge.

Knit 4 rows. Cast off knitwise (on WS).

Buttonhole border

With RS facing, yarn B and 2¾mm (US 2) needles, pick up and knit 75 (81: 87: 93: 99: 105) sts along right front opening edge.

Knit 1 row.

Next row (buttonhole row) (RS): K4, ★yfwd, K2tog, K9 (10: 11: 12: 13: 14), rep from ★ to last 5 sts, yfwd, K2tog, K3.

Knit 2 rows. Cast off knitwise (on WS).

Neck border

With RS facing, yarn A and 2¾mm (US 2) needles, pick up and knit 23 (26: 27: 30: 33: 36) sts up right side of neck, 29 (31: 33: 35: 37: 39) sts from back neck, and 23 (26: 27: 30: 33: 36) sts down left side of neck. 75 (83: 87: 95: 103: 111) sts.

Knit 2 rows.

Work picot cast-off as folls: cast off 2 sts, ★slip st on right needle back onto left needle, cast on 2 sts, cast off 4 sts, rep from ★ to end.

Fasten off.

See info page for finishing instructions, setting in sleeves using the shallow set-in sleeve method.

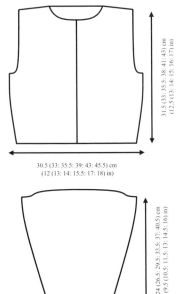

Design number 11

Imp

YARN

Rowan Cotton Glace

	4th	5th	6th	7th	8th	9th	
To fit	2-3	3-4	4-5	6-7	8-9	9-10	yrs
Chest size	22	23	24	26	28	30	in
	(56	58	61	66	71	76	cm)
"Sweet Heart" Sweater							
A Bubbles 724	5	5	6	7	8	9	x 50gm
B Bl Orange 445	2	2	3	3	3	4	x 50gm
"Little Star" Sweater							
A Butter 795	5	5	6	7	8	9	x 50gm
B Pepper 796	2	2	3	3	3	4	x 50gm

NEEDLES

1 pair 2¾mm (no 12) (US 2) needles
1 pair 3¼mm (no 10) (US 3) needles

BUTTONS - 3

TENSION

23 sts and 32 rows to 10 cm measured over stocking stitch using 3¼mm (US 3) needles.

BACK

Cast on 87 (93: 99: 107: 117: 129) sts using 2¾mm (US 2) needles and yarn A.

Knit 2 rows.

Beg with a K row, cont in st st as folls:

Work 2 rows.

Change to 3¼mm (US 3) needles and cont straight until back measures 20 (24: 26.5: 29: 34: 36.5) cm, ending with a WS row.

Shape raglan armholes

Cast off 3 (3: 3: 4: 4: 4) sts at beg of next 2 rows. 81 (87: 93: 99: 109: 121) sts.

Dec 1 st at each end of next 3 (5: 5: 5: 9: 13) rows, then on every foll alt row until 51 (51: 53: 55: 57: 59) sts rem.

Work 1 row, ending with a WS row.

Divide for back opening

Next row (RS): K2tog, K22 (22: 23: 24: 25: 26) and turn, leaving rem sts on a holder.

Work each side of neck separately.

Next row: Cast on and K 3 sts, P to end. 26 (26: 27: 28: 29: 30) sts.

Next row: K2tog, K to end.

Next row: K3, P to end.

Last 2 rows set the border sts.

Keeping 3 border sts in garter st, cont as folls:

Dec 1 st at raglan edge on next and every foll alt row until 16 (16: 17: 18: 19: 20) sts rem.

Work 1 row, ending with a WS row. Cast off.

With RS facing, rejoin yarn to rem sts, K to last 2 sts, K2tog. 26 (26: 27: 28: 29: 30) sts.

Next row (WS): P to last 3 sts, K3.

Last row sets the border sts.

Keeping 3 border sts in garter st, cont as folls:

Work 4 rows, dec 1 st at raglan edge on next and foll alt row. 24 (24: 25: 26: 27: 28) sts.

Next row (buttonhole row) (RS): K1, K2tog, yfwd, K to last 2 sts, K2tog.

Work 7 rows, dec 1 st at raglan edge of 2nd and every foll alt row.

Rep buttonhole hole once more.

Work 7 rows, dec 1 st at raglan edge of 2nd and every foll alt row. 16 (16: 17: 18: 19: 20) sts.

Cast off.

FRONT

Work as for back until front measures 4 cm less than back to beg of raglan shaping, ending with a WS row.

Join in yarn B and place motif as folls:

Next row (RS): K14 (17: 20: 24: 29: 35), starting with chart row 1 and using the INTARSIA method as described on the information page, work 59 sts from chart, K14 (17: 20: 24: 29: 35).

Next row: P14 (17: 20: 24: 29: 35), work across row 2 from chart, P14 (17: 20: 24: 29: 35).

Cont working from chart until chart row 33 completed and AT THE SAME TIME when front matches back to beg of armhole shaping, ending with a WS row, shape armhole as folls:

Shape raglan armholes

Cast off 3 (3: 3: 4: 4: 4) sts at beg of next 2 rows. 81 (87: 93: 99: 109: 121) sts.

Dec 1 st at each end of next 3 (5: 5: 5: 9: 13) rows, then on every foll alt row until 35 (35: 37: 39: 41: 43) sts rem.

Work 1 row, ending with a WS row.

Shape neck

Next row (RS): K2tog, K4 and turn, leaving rem sts on a holder.

Work each side of neck separately.

Next row: P2tog, P3.

Next row: (K2tog) twice.

Next row: P2tog.

Fasten off.

With RS facing, rejoin yarn to rem sts, cast off centre 23 (23: 25: 27: 29: 31) sts, K to last 2 sts, K2tog.

Work to match first side, reversing shapings.

Key □ A ■ B

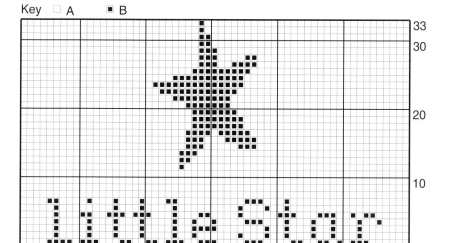

Key □ A ■ B

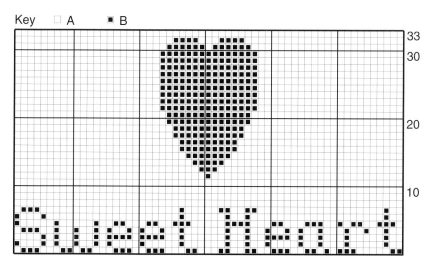

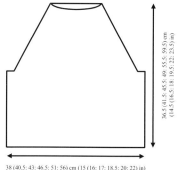

36.5 (41.5: 45.5: 49: 55.5: 59.5) cm
(14.5 (16.5: 18: 19.5: 22: 23.5) in)

21.5 (23: 26: 30.5: 33: 35.5) cm
(8.5 (9: 10: 12: 13: 14) in)

38 (40.5: 43: 46.5: 51: 56) cm (15 (16: 17: 18.5: 20: 22) in)

Archie

YARN
Rowan Cotton Glace

	4th	5th	6th	7th	8th	9th
To fit	2-3	3-4	4-5	6-7	8-9	9-10 yrs
Chest size						
	22	23	24	26	28	30 in
	(56	58	61	66	71	76 cm)
	7	9	10	12	14	16 x 50gm

(Photographed in Steel 798)

NEEDLES
1 pair 2¼mm (no 13) (US 1) needles
1 pair 2¾mm (no 12) (US 2) needles
1 pair 3¼mm (no 10) (US 3) needles

BUTTONS - 2

TENSION
23 sts and 32 rows to 10 cm measured over stocking stitch using 3¼mm (US 3) needles.

BACK
Cast on 85 (93: 99: 107: 117: 129) sts using 2¼mm (US 1) needles.
Beg with a K row, work 8 rows in st st.
Next row (RS): Purl (to form fold line).
Next row: Purl.
Change to 2¾mm (US 2) needles and work in moss st as folls:
Row 1 (RS): K1, *P1, K1, rep from * to end.
Row 2: As row 1.
Work a further 5 rows in moss st, end with RS row.
Next row (WS): Purl.
Change to 3¼mm (US 3) needles and, beg with a K row, cont in st st as folls:
Cont straight until back measures 18.5 (22.5: 25: 27.5: 32.5: 35) cm from fold line row, ending with a WS row.
Shape armholes
Cast off 3 sts at beg of next 2 rows.
79 (87: 93: 101: 111: 123) sts.
Dec 1 st at each end of next 3 (3: 3: 4: 4: 4) rows.
73 (81: 87: 93: 103: 115) sts.
Cont straight until armhole measures 16.5 (17.5: 19: 20: 21.5: 23) cm, ending with a WS row.
Shape shoulders and back neck
Cast off 8 (9: 9: 10: 11: 13) sts at beg of next 2 rows. 57 (63: 69: 73: 81: 89) sts.

SLEEVES (both alike)
Cast on 40 (46: 50: 52: 56: 58) sts using 2¾mm (US 2) needles and yarn B.
Knit 2 rows.
Change to 3¼mm (US 3) needles and, beg with a K row, cont in striped st st as folls:
Row 1 (RS): Using B knit.
Row 2: Using B purl.
Row 3: Using A knit.
Row 4: Using A purl.
Cont in striped st st as set, inc 1 st at each end of next and every foll 6th (6th: 6th: 8th: 8th: 8th) row to 48 (62: 72: 56: 62: 62) sts, then on every foll 4th (4th: 4th: 6th: 6th: 6th) row until there are 66 (70: 76: 80: 86: 92) sts.
Cont straight until sleeve measures 21.5 (23: 26: 30.5: 33: 35.5) cm, ending with a WS row.
Shape raglan
Cast off 3 (3: 3: 4: 4: 4) sts at beg of next 2 rows.
60 (64: 70: 72: 78: 84) sts.
Dec 1 st at each end of next 3 (3: 5: 3: 5: 5) rows, then on every foll alt row until 10 sts rem.
Work 1 row, ending with a WS row.

Left sleeve only
Dec 1 st at both ends of next row.
Cast off 4 sts at beg of next 2 rows.
Right sleeve only
Cast off 5 sts at beg and dec 1 st at end of next row.
Work 1 row. Cast off rem 4 sts.

MAKING UP
PRESS all pieces as described on the info page.
Join raglan seams using back stitch.
Neck border
With RS facing, using yarn B and 2¾mm (US 2) needles, pick up and knit 16 (16: 17: 18: 19: 20) sts across left back neck, 8 sts from left sleeve, 4 sts down left front neck, 23 (23: 25: 27: 29: 31) sts across front neck, 4 sts up right front neck, 8 sts from right sleeve, and 16 (16: 17: 18: 19: 20) sts across right back neck. 79 (79: 83: 87: 91: 95) sts.
Knit 1 row.
Next row (buttonhole row) (RS): K1, K2tog, yfwd, K to end.
Cast off loosely knitwise.
See information page for finishing instructions.

Next row (RS): Cast off 8 (9: 9: 10: 11: 13) sts, K until there are 11 (13: 14: 14: 16: 17) sts on right needle and turn, leaving rem sts on a holder.
Work each side of neck separately.
Cast off 4 sts at beg of next row.
Cast off rem 7 (9: 10: 10: 12: 13) sts.
With RS facing, rejoin yarn to rem sts, cast off centre 19 (19: 23: 25: 27: 29) sts, K to end.
Work to match first side, reversing shapings.

FRONT POCKET LININGS (make 2)
Cast on 25 (27: 27: 29: 29: 31) sts using 3¼mm (US 3) needles.
Beg with a K row, work 31 (33: 35: 37: 39: 41) rows in st st, ending with a RS row.
Break yarn and leave sts on a holder.

FRONT POCKET FLAPS (make 2)
Cast on 27 (29: 29: 31: 31: 33) sts using 3¼mm (US 3) needles.
Work 14 (14: 14: 16: 16: 16) rows in moss st as given for back, ending with a WS row.
Break yarn and leave sts on a holder.

FRONT
Cast on 85 (93: 99: 107: 117: 129) sts using 2¼mm (US 1) needles.
Beg with a K row, work 8 rows in st st.
Next row (RS): Purl (to form fold line).
Next row: Purl.
Change to 2¾mm (US 2) needles and work 3 rows in moss st as given for back, ending with a WS row.
Next row (RS): Moss st 41 (45: 48: 52: 57: 63), cast off 3 sts, moss st to end.
Next row: Moss st to end, casting on 2 sts over those cast off on previous row.
Work a further 2 rows in moss st, ending with a RS row.
Next row (WS): Purl.
Change to 3¼mm (US 3) needles.
Beg with a K row, work 6 rows in st st.
Place pockets
Row 1 (RS): K11 (12: 14: 16: 19: 21), moss st 25 (27: 27: 29: 29: 31), K13 (15: 17: 17: 21: 25), moss st 25 (27: 27: 29: 29: 31), K11 (12: 14: 16: 19: 21).
Row 2: P11 (12: 14: 16: 19: 21), moss st 25 (27: 27: 29: 29: 31), P13 (15: 17: 17: 21: 25), moss st 25 (27: 27: 29: 29: 31), P11 (12: 14: 16: 19: 21).
Rep last 2 rows 14 (15: 16: 17: 18: 19) times more.
Next row (RS): K11 (12: 14: 16: 19: 21), cast off next 25 (27: 27: 29: 29: 31) sts in moss st, K until there are 13 (15: 17: 17: 21: 25) sts on right needle after cast-off, cast off next 25 (27: 27: 29: 29: 31) sts in moss st, K to end.
Next row: P11 (12: 14: 16: 19: 21), P across 25 (27: 27: 29: 29: 31) sts of first pocket lining, P13 (15: 17: 17: 21: 25), P across 25 (27: 27: 29: 29: 31) sts of second pocket lining, P to end.
Join pocket flaps
Next row (RS): K10 (11: 13: 15: 18: 20), holding WS of first pocket flap against RS of front, K tog first st of pocket flap and next st of front, K tog rem 26 (28: 28: 30: 30: 32) sts of pocket flap with next 26 (28: 28: 30: 30: 32) sts of front in same way, K11 (13: 15: 15: 19: 23), holding WS of second pocket flap against RS of front, K tog first st of pocket flap tog with next st of front, K tog rem 26 (28: 28: 30: 30: 32) sts of pocket flap with next 26 (28: 28: 30: 30: 32) sts of front in same way, K to end.

Beg with a P row, cont in st st as folls:
Cont straight until front matches back to beg of armhole shaping, ending with a WS row.
Shape armholes
Cast off 3 sts at beg of next 2 rows.
79 (87: 93: 101: 111: 123) sts.
Dec 1 st at each end of next 3 (3: 3: 4: 4: 4) rows.
73 (81: 87: 93: 103: 115) sts.
Cont straight until armhole measures 6 (7: 8: 9: 10: 11) cm, ending with a WS row.
Shape front opening borders
Row 1 (RS): K31 (35: 38: 41: 46: 52), (P1, K1) 5 times, P1, K31 (35: 38: 41: 46: 52).
Row 2: P30 (34: 37: 40: 45: 51), (K1, P1) 6 times, K1, P30 (34: 37: 40: 45: 51).
Row 3: K29 (33: 36: 39: 44: 50), (P1, K1) 7 times, P1, K29 (33: 36: 39: 44: 50).
Row 4: P28 (32: 35: 38: 43: 49), (K1, P1) 8 times, K1, P28 (32: 35: 38: 43: 49).
Row 5: K27 (31: 34: 37: 42: 48), (P1, K1) 9 times, P1, K27 (31: 34: 37: 42: 48).
Row 6: P26 (30: 33: 36: 41: 47), (K1, P1) 10 times, K1, P26 (30: 33: 36: 41: 47).
Divide for front opening
Next row (RS): K25 (29: 32: 35: 40: 46), (P1, K1) 5 times, P1, and turn, leaving rem sts on a holder.
36 (40: 43: 46: 51: 57) sts.
Work each side of neck separately.
Next row: (P1, K1) 6 times, P to end.
Next row: K to last 13 sts, (P1, K1) 6 times, P1.
Next row: (P1, K1) 7 times, P to end.
Rep last 2 rows until front matches back to start of shoulder shaping, ending with a WS row.
Shape shoulder
Cast off 8 (9: 9: 10: 11: 13) sts at beg of next and foll alt row, then 7 (9: 10: 10: 12: 13) sts at beg of foll alt row.
Work 1 row.
Break yarn and leave rem 13 (13: 15: 16: 17: 18) sts on a holder.
With RS facing, rejoin yarn to rem sts and cont as folls:
Next row (RS): P2tog, (K1, P1) 5 times, K to end. 36 (40: 43: 46: 51: 57) sts.
Next row: P to last 12 sts, (K1, P1) 6 times.
Next row: P1, (K1, P1) 6 times, K to end.
Next row: P to last 14 sts, (K1, P1) 7 times.
Rep last 2 rows until front matches back to start of shoulder shaping, ending with a RS row.
Shape shoulder
Cast off 8 (9: 9: 10: 11: 13) sts at beg of next and foll alt row, then 7 (9: 10: 10: 12: 13) sts at beg of foll alt row.
Do NOT break yarn.
Leave rem 13 (13: 15: 16: 17: 18) sts on a holder and set aside ball of yarn - this will be used for hood.

RIGHT SLEEVE
Cast on 45 (47: 49: 53: 55: 59) sts using 2¾mm (US 2) needles.
Work 6 rows in moss st as given for back, ending with a WS row.
Change to 3¼mm (US 3) needles and, beg with a K row, cont in st st, shaping sides by inc 1 st at each end of 3rd (3rd: 3rd: 5th: 5th: 5th) and every foll 4th row until there are 65 (71: 79: 93: 99: 107) sts.
4th, 5th and 6th sizes only
Inc 1 st at each end of every foll alt row until there are 77 (81: 87) sts.
All sizes
Cont straight until sleeve measures 21.5 (23: 26: 30.5: 33: 35.5) cm, ending with a WS row.

Shape top
Cast off 3 sts at beg of next 2 rows.
71 (75: 81: 87: 93: 101) sts.
Dec 1 st at each end of next and foll 2 (2: 2: 3: 3: 3) alt rows.
Work 1 row, ending with a WS row.
Cast off rem 65 (69: 75: 79: 85: 93) sts.

SLEEVE POCKET LINING
Cast on 19 (19: 21: 21: 23: 23) sts using 3¼mm (US 3) needles.
Beg with a K row, work 21 (21: 23: 23: 25: 25) rows in st st, ending with a RS row.
Break yarn and leave sts on a holder.

SLEEVE POCKET FLAP
Cast on 21 (21: 23: 23: 25: 25) sts using 3¼mm (US 3) needles.
Work 10 (10: 10: 12: 12: 12) rows in moss st as given for back, ending with a WS row.
Break yarn and leave sts on a holder.

LEFT SLEEVE
Work as for right sleeve until sleeve measures 11 (12: 13: 15: 17: 18) cm, ending with a WS row.
Place markers either side of centre 19 (19: 21: 21: 23: 23) sts.
Keeping increases correct as set, cont as folls:
Next row (RS): K to first marker (working inc if appropriate), (P1, K1) 9 (9: 10: 10: 11: 11) times, P1, K to end (working inc if appropriate).
This row sets position of moss st worked over centre 19 (19: 21: 21: 23: 23) sts between markers.
Working increases as for right sleeve, work a further 19 (19: 21: 21: 23: 23) rows in st st with centre sts between markers in moss st, ending with a WS row.
Next row (RS): K to first marker (working inc if appropriate), cast off centre 19 (19: 21: 21: 23: 23) sts in moss st, K to end (working inc if appropriate).
Next row: P to first marker, P across 19 (19: 21: 21: 23: 23) sts of pocket lining, P to end.
Join pocket flap
Next row (RS): K to within 1 st of first marker (working inc if appropriate), holding WS of pocket flap against RS of sleeve, K tog first st of pocket flap and next st of sleeve, K tog rem 20 (20: 22: 22: 24: 24) sts of pocket flap and next 20 (20: 22: 22: 24: 24) sts of sleeve in same way, K to end (working inc if appropriate).
Beg with a P row, cont in st st and complete as for right sleeve.

MAKING UP
PRESS all pieces as described on the information page.
Join shoulder seams using back stitch.
Hood
With RS facing, using ball of yarn left at right front neck edge and 3¼mm (US 3) needles, patt across 13 (13: 15: 16: 17: 18) sts of right front, pick up and knit 27 (27: 31: 33: 35: 37) sts across back neck placing marker on centre st, then patt across 13 (13: 15: 16: 17: 18) sts of left front.
53 (53: 61: 65: 69: 73) sts.
Now work in moss st as set by front opening edge sts as folls:
Work 1 row.
Next row (RS) (inc): Moss to marked st, M1, K1, M1, moss st to end.
Rep last 2 rows 10 times more.
75 (75: 83: 87: 91: 95) sts.
Work 3 rows.

Next row (RS) (inc): Moss to marked st, M1, K1, M1, moss st to end.
Rep last 4 rows 5 times more.
87 (87: 95: 99: 103: 107) sts.
Cont straight until hood measures 23 (24: 25: 26: 27: 28) cm, ending with a WS row.
Next row (RS) (dec): Moss st to within 2 sts of marked centre st, work 2 tog, K1, work 2 tog tbl, moss st to end.
Work 1 row.
Rep last 2 rows twice more, dec 1 st at centre of last row. 80 (80: 88: 92: 96: 100) sts.
Next row (RS): Moss st 40 (40: 44: 46: 48: 50) and turn.
Fold hood in half with **WS** facing and, using a spare needle, cast off sts from each needle tog to form hood seam.

Button loops (make 2)
Cast on 14 sts using 3¼mm (US 3) needles.
Cast off.
Fold button loops in half and sew to inside of front opening edge as in photograph. Attach buttons to correspond.

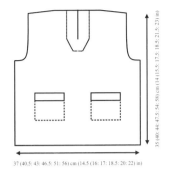

Fold first 8 rows of front and back to inside along fold line and slip stitch in place. Make a twisted cord approx 150 cm long and knot ends. Thread cord through hem casing and tie ends at front.
See information page for finishing instructions, setting-in sleeves using the shallow set-in method.

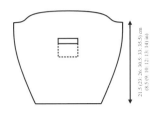

Design number 13

Chill

YARN
Rowan DK Soft

	4th	5th	6th	7th	8th	9th	
To fit							
	2-3	3-4	4-5	6-7	8-9	9-10	yrs
Chest size							
	22	23	24	26	28	30	in
	(56	58	61	66	71	76	cm)
	4	4	5	6	7	8	x 50gm

(photographed in Chalk 170)

NEEDLES
1 pair 5mm (no 6) (US 8) needles
1 pair 5½mm (no 5) (US 9) needles

TENSION
26 sts and 32 rows to 10 cm measured over pattern using 5½mm (US 9) needles.

BACK
Cast on 97 (105: 111: 119: 131: 145) sts using 5mm (US 8) needles.
Row 1 (RS): K1, *P1, K1, rep from * to end.
Row 2: K1, *slip next st purlwise with yarn at back of work, K1, rep from * to end.
These 2 rows form patt.
Patt a further 4 rows.

Change to 5½mm (US 9) needles.
Cont in patt until back measures 18.5 (22.5: 25: 30.5: 35.5: 38) cm from cast-on edge, ending with a WS row.
Shape armholes
Keeping patt correct, cast off 3 (3: 3: 4: 4: 4) sts at beg of next 2 rows. 91 (99: 105: 111: 123: 137) sts.
Dec 1 st at each end of next and foll 2 (2: 2: 3: 3: 3) alt rows. 85 (93: 99: 103: 115: 129) sts.
Cont straight until armhole measures 16.5 (17.5: 19: 20: 21.5: 23) cm, ending with a WS row.
Shape shoulders and back neck
Cast off 8 (9: 10: 10: 12: 14) sts at beg of next 2 rows. 69 (75: 79: 83: 91: 101) sts.
Next row (RS): Cast off 8 (9: 10: 10: 12: 14) sts, patt until there are 12 (14: 14: 15: 15: 17) sts on right needle and turn, leaving rem sts on a holder.
Work each side of neck separately.
Cast off 4 sts at beg of next row.
Cast off rem 8 (10: 10: 11: 11: 13) sts.
With RS facing, rejoin yarn to rem sts, cast off centre 29 (29: 31: 33: 37: 39) sts, patt to end.
Work to match first side, reversing shapings.

FRONT
Work as for back until 10 (12: 12: 20: 20: 22) rows less have been worked than on back to start of shoulder shaping, ending with a WS row.
Shape neck
Next row (RS): Patt 34 (38: 41: 43: 49: 56) sts and turn, leaving rem sts on a holder.
Work each side of neck separately.
Cast off 4 sts at beg of next row.
30 (34: 37: 39: 45: 52) sts.
Dec 1 st at neck edge of next 6 (6: 6: 6: 8: 8) rows, then on foll 0 (0: 1: 2: 2: 3) alt rows.
24 (28: 30: 31: 35: 41) sts.
Work 2 (4: 2: 8: 6: 6) rows.
Shape shoulder
Cast off 8 (9: 10: 10: 12: 14) sts at beg of next and foll alt row.
Work 1 row.

Cast off rem 8 (10: 10: 11: 11: 13) sts.
With RS facing, rejoin yarn to rem sts, cast off centre 17 sts, patt to end.
Work to match first side, reversing shapings.

SLEEVES (both alike)
Cast on 49 (53: 55: 61: 65: 67) sts using 5½mm (US 9) needles.
Beg with a 1st row, work in patt as for back for 7.5 (7.5: 8.5: 8.5: 9.5: 9.5) cm, end with a WS row.
Cont in patt, inc 1 st at each end of next and every foll alt row to 69 (71: 75: 69: 69: 73) sts, then on every foll 4th row until there are 85 (91: 99: 105: 111: 119) sts, taking inc sts into patt.
Cont straight until sleeve measures 27 (28.5: 32.5: 36.5: 40.5: 43) cm from cast-on edge, ending with a WS row.
Shape top
Keeping patt correct, cast off 3 (3: 3: 4: 4: 4) sts at beg of next 2 rows. 79 (85: 93: 97: 103: 111) sts.
Dec 1 st at each end of next and foll 2 (2: 2: 3: 3: 3) alt rows. 73 (79: 87: 89: 95: 103) sts.
Work 1 row. Cast off loosely in patt.

MAKING UP
PRESS all pieces as described on the info page.
Join right shoulder seam using back stitch.
Neck border
With RS facing and 5½mm (US 9) needles, pick up and knit 16 (18: 18: 24: 24: 26) sts down left front neck, 17 sts across front neck, 16 (18: 18: 24: 24: 26) sts up right front neck, and 38 (38: 40: 42: 46: 48) sts across back neck.
87 (91: 93: 107: 111: 117) sts.
Beg with a WS row, cont in patt as for back for 7.5 (7.5: 8.5: 8.5: 9.5: 9.5) cm.
Cast off loosely in patt.
Join left shoulder and neck border seam using back stitch. Set in sleeves using the shallow set-in sleeve method described on the information page. See info page for finishing instructions.
Fold 5.5 (5.5: 6.5: 6.5: 7.5: 7.5) cm cuff to RS.

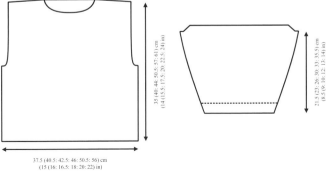

Sport

YARN

Rowan Handknit DK Cotton

	4th	5th	6th	7th	8th	9th	
To fit							
	2-3	3-4	4-5	6-7	8-9	9-10	yrs
Chest size							
	22	23	24	26	28	30	in
	(56	58	61	66	71	76	cm)
	5	6	7	8	9	10	x 50gm

(photographed in Fruit Salad 203)

NEEDLES

1 pair 3¼mm (no 10) (US 3) needles
1 pair 4mm (no 8) (US 6) needles

BUTTONS – 5 (5: 5: 6: 6: 6)

TENSION

20 sts and 28 rows to 10 cm measured over flattened rib pattern using 4mm (US 6) needles.

BACK

Cast on 61 (65: 71: 79: 87: 91) sts using 3¼mm (US 3) needles.
Row 1 (RS) : K2 (0: 2: 1: 0: 2), P2 (1: 2: 2: 2: 2), *K3, P2, rep from * to last 2 (4: 2: 1: 0: 2) sts, K2 (3: 2: 1: 0: 2), P0 (1: 0: 0: 0: 0).
Row 2: P2 (0: 2: 1: 0: 2), K2 (1: 2: 2: 2: 2), *P3, K2, rep from * to last 2 (4: 2: 1: 0: 2) sts, P2 (3: 2: 1: 0: 2), K0 (1: 0: 0: 0: 0).
These 2 rows form the pattern.
Rep these 2 rows 4 times more, ending with a WS row.
Change to 4mm (US 6) needles and, keeping patt correct, cont until work measures 19 (20: 22: 23.5: 26: 27) cm, from cast-on edge, ending with a WS row.
Shape armholes
Keeping patt correct, cast off 5 (5: 5: 6: 6: 6) sts at beg of next 2 rows. 51 (55: 61: 67: 75: 79) sts.
Cont without further shaping until work measures 15 (16: 17: 18: 19: 20) cm from beg of armhole shaping, ending with a WS row.
Shape shoulders and back neck
Cast off 5 (6: 6: 7: 8: 8) sts at beg of next 2 rows. 41 (43: 49: 53: 59: 63) sts.
Next row (RS): Cast off 5 (6: 6: 7: 8: 8) sts, patt until there are 9 (9: 11: 12: 13: 13) sts on right

needle and turn, leaving rem sts on a holder.
Work each side of neck separately.
Cast off 4 sts at beg of next row.
Cast off rem 5 (5: 7: 8: 9: 9) sts.
With RS facing, rejoin yarn to rem sts, cast off centre 13 (13: 15: 15: 17: 21) sts, patt to end.
Work to match first side, reversing shaping.

LEFT FRONT

Cast on 37 (39: 42: 47: 51: 53) sts using 3¼mm (US 3) needles.
Row 1 (RS): K2 (0: 2: 1: 0: 2), P2 (1: 2: 2: 2: 2), *K3, P2, rep from * to last 8 (8: 8: 9: 9: 9) sts, K3, P1, (K1, P1) twice, K0 (0: 0: 1: 1: 1).
Row 2: K0 (0: 0: 1: 1: 1), (P1, K1) twice, P4, K2, *P3, K2, rep from * to last 2 (4: 2: 1: 0: 2) sts, P2 (3: 2: 1: 0: 0), K0 (1: 0: 0: 0: 0).
These 2 rows form the pattern.
Keeping 5 (5: 5: 6: 6: 6) sts at centre front in moss st for button band, cont as folls:
Work a further 8 rows.
Change to 4mm (US 6) needles and, keeping patt correct, cont until left front matches back to beg of armhole shaping, ending with a WS row.
Shape armholes
Keeping patt correct, cast off 5 (5: 5: 6: 6: 6) sts at beg of next row. 32 (34: 37: 41: 45: 47) sts.
Cont in patt until left front is 11 (13: 13: 15: 15: 17) rows shorter than back to start of shoulder shaping, ending with a RS row.
Shape neck
Next row (WS): Patt 9 (9: 9: 10: 10: 11) sts, leave these sts on a holder for front neck, patt to end. 23 (25: 28: 31: 35: 36) sts.
Cont in patt, dec 1 st at neck edge of next 7 (6: 7: 6: 7: 8) rows, then on every foll alt row until 15 (17: 19: 22: 25: 25) sts rem.
Work 1 (2: 1: 2: 1: 2) rows, ending with a WS row.
Shape shoulder
Cast off 5 (6: 6: 7: 8: 8) sts at beg of next and foll alt row.
Work 1 row.
Cast off rem 5 (5: 7: 8: 9: 9) sts.
Mark positions for 5 (5: 5: 6: 6: 6) buttons along left front opening edge - lowest to come 5 cm up from cast-on edge, last button 1 cm below neck shaping and rem buttons evenly spaced between.

RIGHT FRONT

Cast on 37 (39: 42: 47: 51: 53) sts using 3¼mm (US 3) needles.
Row 1 (RS): K0 (0: 0: 1: 1: 1), (P1, K1) twice, P1, *K3, P2, rep from * to last 2 (4: 2: 1: 0: 2) sts, K2 (3: 2: 1: 0: 2), P0 (1: 0: 0: 0: 0).
Row 2 : P2 (0: 2: 1: 0: 2), K2 (1: 2: 2: 2: 2), *P3, K2, rep from * to last 8 (8: 8: 9: 9: 9) sts, P4, (K1, P1) twice, K0 (0: 0: 1: 1: 1).
These 2 rows form the pattern.
Keeping 5 (5: 5: 6: 6: 6) sts at centre front in moss st for buttonhole band, complete to match left front, reversing all shaping, and with the addition of 5 (5: 5: 6: 6: 6) buttonholes to correspond with positions marked for buttons, worked as folls:
Buttonhole row (RS): Moss st 2, yrn, patt 2 tog, patt to end.

SLEEVES (both alike)

Cast on 33 (33: 35: 37: 39: 41) sts using 3¼mm (US 3) needles.
Row 1 (RS) : P0 (0: 1: 0: 0: 0), K3 (3: 3: 0: 1: 2), *P2, K3, rep from * to last 0 (0: 1: 2: 3: 4) sts, P0 (0: 1: 2: 2: 2), K0 (0: 0: 0: 1: 2).

Row 2: K0 (0: 1: 0: 0: 0), P3 (3: 3: 0: 1: 2), *K2, P3, rep from * to last 0 (0: 1: 2: 3: 4) sts, K0 (0: 1: 2: 2: 2), P0 (0: 0: 0: 1: 2).
These 2 rows form the pattern and are rep throughout.
Work a further 8 rows in patt, inc 1 st at each end of 5th of these rows. 35 (35: 37: 39: 41: 43) sts.
Change to 4mm (US 6) needles.
Cont in rib patt, shaping sleeve seam by inc 1 st at each end of next and every foll 4th row to 61 (65: 69: 51: 57: 65) sts, taking inc sts into patt.
4th, 5th and 6th sizes only
Cont without further shaping until work measures 26.5 (29: 32) cm from cast-on edge, ending with a WS row.
Cast off evenly in rib patt.
7th, 8th and 9th sizes only
Cont in patt, shaping sides by inc 1 st at each end of every foll 6th row to – (–: –: 73: 77: 81) sts.
Work straight sleeve measures – (–: –: 36.5: 40: 43.5) cm, ending with a WS row.
Cast off evenly in rib patt.

MAKING UP

PRESS all pieces as described on the information page.
Join both shoulder seams using back stitch.
Collar
With RS facing and using 3¼mm (US 3) needles, slip sts from right front holder onto right needle, rejoin yarn and pick up and knit 12 (14: 16: 18: 20: 19) sts up right front neck, 21 (21: 23: 23: 25: 29) sts across back neck, 12 (15: 16: 19: 20: 20) down left front neck, then patt across sts from left front holder. 63 (68: 73: 80: 85: 90) sts.
Row 1 (RS of collar, WS of body): Moss st 5 (5: 5: 6: 6: 6), *K3, P2, rep from * to last 8 (8: 8: 9: 9: 9) sts, K3, moss st to end.
Row 2: Moss st 5 (5: 5: 6: 6: 6), *P3, K2, rep from * to last 8 (8: 8: 9: 9: 9) sts, P3, moss st to end.
Rep last 2 rows for 7 (7: 7: 9: 9: 9) cm.
Cast off in patt.
Set sleeve into armhole using the square set-in method described on the information page.
Sew on buttons to correspond with buttonholes.
See information page for finishing instructions.

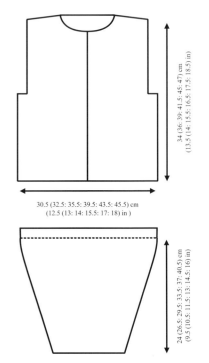

Design number 15

Maisie

YARN
Rowan 4 ply Cotton

	1st	2nd	
To fit	0-6	6-12	mths
Chest size	16	18	in
	(41	46	cm)
	2	3	x 50gm

3rd	4th	5th	6th	7th	8th	9th	
To fit							
1-2	2-3	3-4	4-5	6-7	8-9	9-10	yrs
Chest size							
20	22	23	24	26	28	30	in
(51	56	58	61	66	71	76	cm)
3	4	4	5	5	6	7	x 50gm

(photographed in Tear 116)

NEEDLES
1 pair 2¼mm (no 13) (US 1) needles
1 pair 3mm (no 11) (US 2/3) needles

BUTTONS - 5 (5: 5: 5: 5: 6: 6: 6: 6)

TENSION
28 sts and 36 rows to 10 cm measured over st st using 3mm (US 2/3) needles.

BACK
Cast on 71 (81: 75: 79: 87: 93: 101: 113: 119) sts using 2¼mm (US 1) needles.
Row 1 (RS) : K1, ★ P1, K1, rep from ★ to end.
Row 2 : As row 1.
These 2 rows form moss st.
Work a further 4 (4: 4: 6: 6: 8: 8: 8: 8) rows in moss st.
Change to 3mm (US 2/3) needles and, beg with a K row, cont in st st as folls:
1st and 2nd sizes only
Cont straight until back measures 11.5 (13) cm, ending with a WS row.
3rd, 4th, 5th, 6th, 7th, 8th and 9th sizes only
Inc 1 st at each end of – (–: 7th: 7th: 5th: 5th: 3rd: 5th: 5th) and every foll – (–: 12th: 12th: 12th: 14th: 14th: 14th: 14th) row until there are
– (–: 81: 85: 93: 99: 109: 121: 127) sts.
Cont straight until back measures – (–: 16.5: 16.5: 17: 18.5: 20: 22: 23) cm, ending with a WS row.

All sizes
Shape armholes
Cast off 6 (6: 6: 7: 7: 7: 8: 8: 8) sts at beg of next 2 rows. 59 (69: 69: 71: 79: 85: 93: 105: 111) sts.
Cont straight until armhole measures 11.5 (12.5: 14: 15: 16: 17: 18: 19: 20) cm, ending with a WS row.
Shape shoulders and back neck
Cast off 5 (7: 6: 7: 8: 9: 9: 11: 11) sts at beg of next 2 rows.
49 (51: 57: 57: 63: 67: 75: 83: 89) sts.
Next row (RS): Cast off 5 (7: 6: 7: 8: 9: 9: 11: 11) sts, K until there are 9 (10: 11: 10: 11: 12: 14: 15: 16) sts on right needle and turn, leaving rem sts on a holder.
Work each side of neck separately.
Cast off 4 sts at beg of next row.
Cast off rem 5 (6: 7: 6: 7: 8: 10: 11: 12) sts.
With RS facing, rejoin yarn to rem sts, cast off centre 21 (21: 23: 23: 25: 25: 29: 31: 35) sts, K to end.
Work to match first side, reversing shaping.

POCKET LININGS (make two)
Cast on 19 (19: 21: 21: 23: 23: 25: 27: 27) sts using 3mm (US 2/3) needles.
Beg with a K row, work 18 (18: 26: 26: 30: 30: 36: 36: 36) rows in st st, ending with a WS row.
Break yarn and leave sts on a holder.

LEFT FRONT
Cast on 41 (45: 43: 45: 49: 51: 55: 61: 65) sts using 2¼mm (US 1) needles.
Work 5 (5: 5: 7: 7: 9: 9: 9: 9) rows in moss st as given for back, inc 0 (1: 0: 0: 0: 1: 1: 1: 0) st at beg of last row.
41 (46: 43: 45: 49: 52: 56: 62: 65) sts.
Next row (WS): Moss st 5, slip these sts onto a holder for button border, moss st to end.
36 (41: 38: 40: 44: 47: 51: 57: 60) sts.
Change to 3mm (US 2/3) needles and, beg with a K row, cont in st st as folls:
1st and 2nd sizes only
Work 18 rows straight, ending with a WS row.
Place pocket
Next row (RS): K9 (12), slip next 19 sts onto a holder and, in their place, K across 19 sts of first pocket lining, K to end.
3rd, 4th, 5th, 6th, 7th, 8th and 9th sizes only
Inc 1 st at beg of – (–: 7th: 7th: 5th: 5th: 3rd: 5th: 5th) and every foll – (–: 12th: 12th: 12th: 14th: 14th: 14th: 14th) row until there are – (–: 41: 43: 47: 50: 55: 61: 64) sts **AT THE SAME TIME,** when work measures – (–: 9: 9: 11: 11: 13: 13: 13) cm, **place pocket** as folls:
Next row: K– (–: 10: 11: 13: 14: 15: 17: 19), slip next – (–: 21: 21: 23: 23: 25: 27: 27) sts onto a holder and, in their place, K across the sts of first pocket lining, K to end.
All sizes
Beg with a P row, cont in st st until left front matches back to beg of armhole shaping, ending with a WS row.
Shape armhole
Cast off 6 (6: 6: 7: 7: 7: 8: 8: 8) sts at beg of next row. 30 (35: 35: 36: 40: 43: 47: 53: 56) sts.
Cont straight until left front is 9 (11: 13: 13: 15: 15: 19: 19: 21) rows shorter than back to start of shoulder shaping, ending with a RS row.
Shape neck
Next row (WS): Cast off 7 (7: 7: 7: 7: 7: 7: 8: 8) sts at beg of next row, and 3 (3: 3: 3: 3: 3: 3: 4: 4) sts at beg of foll alt row.
20 (25: 25: 26: 30: 33: 37: 41: 44) sts.

Dec 1 st at neck edge on next 4 (4: 4: 4: 5: 5: 5: 5: 6) rows, then on every foll alt row until 15 (20: 19: 20: 23: 26: 28: 33: 34) sts rem.
Work 0 (2: 2: 2: 3: 3: 3: 5: 4) rows, ending with a WS row.
Shape shoulder
Cast off 5 (7: 6: 7: 8: 9: 9: 11: 11) sts at beg of next and foll alt row.
Work 1 row.
Cast off rem 5 (6: 7: 6: 7: 8: 10: 11: 12) sts.

RIGHT FRONT
Cast on 41 (45: 43: 45: 49: 51: 55: 61: 65) sts using 2¼mm (US 1) needles and work 2 rows in moss st as given for back.
Next row (buttonhole row): Moss st 2, yon, work 2tog, moss st to end.
Work a further 2 (2: 2: 4: 4: 6: 6: 6: 6) rows in moss st as for back, inc 0 (1: 0: 0: 0: 1: 1: 1: 0) st at end of last row.
41 (46: 43: 45: 49: 52: 56: 62: 65) sts.
Next row (WS): Moss st to last 5 sts and turn, leaving rem 5 sts on a holder for buttonhole border.
36 (41: 38: 40: 44: 47: 51: 57: 60) sts.
Change to 3mm (US 2/3) needles and, beg with a K row, cont in st st as folls:
1st and 2nd sizes only
Work 18 rows straight, ending with a WS row.
Place pocket
Next row (RS): K8 (9), slip next 19 sts onto a holder and, in their place, K across 19 sts of second pocket lining, K to end.
3rd, 4th, 5th, 6th, 7th, 8th and 9th sizes only
Inc 1 st at end of – (–: 7th: 7th: 5th: 5th: 3rd: 5th: 5th) and every foll – (–: 12th: 12th: 12th: 14th: 14th: 14th: 14th) row until there are – (–: 41: 43: 47: 50: 55: 61: 64) sts **AT THE SAME TIME,** when work measures – (–: 9: 9: 11: 11: 13: 13: 13) cm, **place pocket** as folls:
Next row: K to last – (–: 31: 32: 36: 37: 40: 44: 46) sts, slip next – (–: 21: 21: 23: 23: 25: 27: 27) sts onto a holder and, in their place, K across the sts of second pocket lining, K to end.
All sizes
Beg with a P row, cont in st st until right front matches back to beg of armhole shaping, ending with a WS row.
Complete to match left front, reversing all shaping.

SLEEVES (both alike)
Cast on 39 (41: 43: 45: 47: 47: 51: 53: 57) sts using 2¼mm (US 1) needles and work 6 (6: 6: 8: 8: 10: 10: 10: 10) rows in moss st as given for back.
Change to 3mm (US 2/3) needles.
Beg with a K row, work in st st, shaping sleeve seam by inc 1 st at each end of 7th and every foll 4th row to 51 (63: 63: 81: 81: 89: 99: 105: 111) sts, then on every alt row to 65 (71: 79: 85: 89: 95: 101: 107: 113) sts.
Cont without further shaping until sleeve measures 15 (19: 20.5: 27: 29.5: 32: 37: 40: 43) cm, ending with a WS row.
Cast off evenly.

MAKING UP
PRESS all pieces as described on the information page.
Join both shoulder seams using back stitch.
Button border
Slip sts from left front holder onto 2¼mm (US 1) needles and rejoin yarn with RS facing.

Cont in moss st as set until border, when slightly stretched, fits up left front opening edge to neck shaping, ending with a WS row.
Leave sts on a holder.
Slip st border in place.
Mark positions for 5 (5: 5: 5: 5: 6: 6: 6: 6) buttons on this border – the first button level with buttonhole already worked in right front, the last one will be in neckband, 1 cm above start of neck shaping, and rem buttons evenly spaced between.

Buttonhole border
Work as for button border, rejoining yarn with WS facing and with the addition of a further 3 (3: 3: 3: 3: 4: 4: 4: 4) buttonholes to correspond with positions marked for buttons, worked as folls:
Buttonhole row (RS): Moss st 2, yon, work 2tog, moss st 1.
Do not break yarn. Slip st border in place.
Neckband
With RS facing and using 2¼mm (US 1) needles, patt across 5 sts of buttonhole border, pick up and knit 19 (20: 22: 22: 25: 25: 28: 29: 32) sts up right side of neck, 29 (29: 31: 31: 33: 33: 37: 39: 43) sts from back, 19 (20: 22: 22: 25: 25: 28: 29: 32) sts down left side of neck and patt across 5 sts of button border.
77 (79: 85: 85: 93: 93: 103: 107: 117) sts.
Work 3 (3: 3: 3: 3: 3: 3: 5: 5) rows in moss st as for back.
Next row (Buttonhole row): Moss st 2, yon, work 2tog, moss st to end.
Work a further 2 rows in moss st.
Cast off evenly in moss st.
Pocket tops
Slip 19 (19: 21: 21: 23: 23: 25: 27: 27) sts from pocket holder onto 2¼mm (US 1) needles and rejoin yarn with RS facing.
Work 6 rows in moss st. Cast off evenly in patt.
Slip st pocket top and lining neatly into place.
Set sleeve into armhole using the square set-in method described on the information page.
Sew on buttons to correspond with buttonholes.
See information page for finishing instructions.

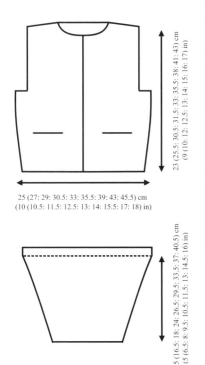

23 (25.5: 30.5: 31.5: 33: 35.5: 38: 41: 43) cm
(9 (10: 12: 12.5: 13: 14: 15: 16: 17) in)

25 (27: 29: 30.5: 33: 35.5: 39: 43: 45.5) cm
(10 (10.5: 11.5: 12.5: 13: 14: 15.5: 17: 18) in)

12.5 (16.5: 18: 24: 26.5: 29.5: 33.5: 37: 40.5) cm
(5 (6.5: 8: 9.5: 10.5: 11.5: 13: 14.5: 16) in)

Design number 16

Hide cushion

YARN
Rowan D.K. Soft
First Colourway

A	Chalk	170	2	x 50gm
B	Luna	173	2	x 50gm

Second Colourway

A	Luna	173	2	x 50gm
B	Chalk	170	2	x 50gm

NEEDLES
1 pair 4mm (no 8) (US 6) needles

TENSION
23 sts and 32 rows to 10 cm measured over patterned st st using 4mm (US 6) needles.

MEASUREMENTS
Finished cushion is approx 41 cm (16 in) square.

FRONT and BACK (both alike)
Cast on 94 sts using 4mm (US 6) needles and yarn A.
Using the **intarsia** technique described on the information page, starting and ending rows as indicated on chart for blanket, and beginning with chart row 11, work 132 rows in patt from chart, beg with a K row.
Cast off.

MAKING UP
PRESS pieces as described on the information page.
With right sides facing, sew pieces together along 3 sides using back stitch.
Turn right side out and insert cushion pad.
Sew remaining side closed.
See information page for finishing instructions.

Design number 17

Hide blanket

YARN

Rowan D.K. Soft

A	Chalk	170	2	x	50gm
B	Luna	173	2	x	50gm

NEEDLES

1 pair 3¼mm (no 10) (US 3) needles
1 pair 4mm (no 8) (US 6) needles

TENSION

23 sts and 32 rows to 10 cm measured over patterned st st using 4mm (US 6) needles.

MEASUREMENTS

Finished blanket is approx 57 cm (22½ in) wide by 70 cm (27½ in) long.

Pattern note: As row end edges of blanket form the actual finished edges of this design, it is important that these edges are kept neat. Therefore, all new balls of yarn should be joined in at natural colour change breaks within the blanket or inside the moss st borders.

BLANKET

Cast on 131 sts using 3¼mm (US 3) needles and yarn A and work in patt from chart, setting sts as folls:

Row 1 (RS): K1, *P1, K1, rep from * to end.
Row 2: As row 1.
Cont in patt from chart, work a further 4 rows in moss st.
Change to 4mm (US 6) needles.
Row 7 (RS): Moss st 5, K to last 5 sts, moss st 5.
Row 8: Moss st 5, P to last 5 sts, moss st 5.
Joining in and breaking off colours as required, and using the **intarsia** technique described on the information page, cont in patterned st st from chart until chart row 216 has been completed, **at the same time** working 5 sts at each side edge in moss st as indicated.
Break yarn B and complete using yarn A only.
Row 217 (RS): Moss st 5, K to last 5 sts, moss st 5.
Row 218: Moss st 5, P to last 5 sts, moss st 5.
Change to 3¼mm (US 3) needles and work 6 rows in moss st from chart, ending with a WS row.
Cast off evenly in moss st.

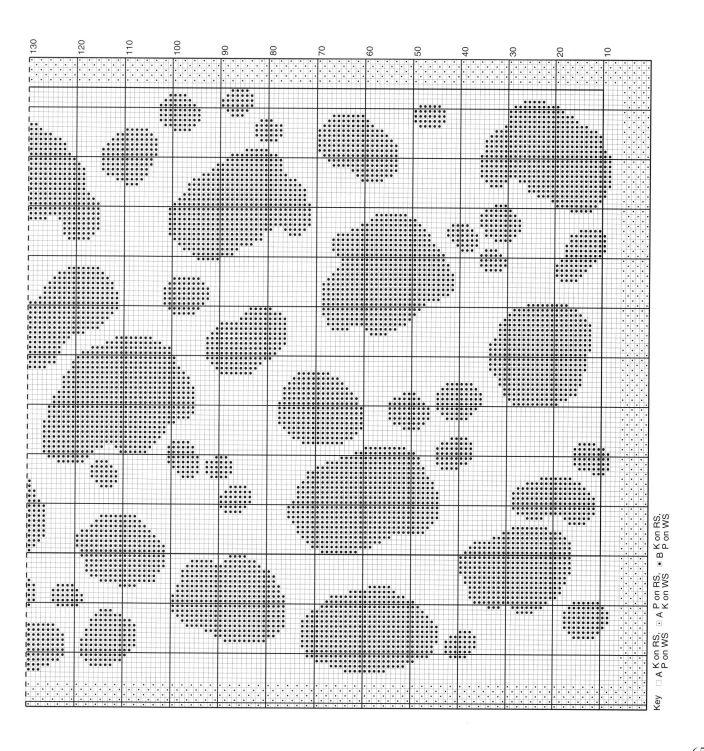

Key
☐ A K on RS, A P on WS
⊡ A P on RS, A K on WS
⊡ B K on RS, B P on WS

Daisy

YARN

Rowan Cotton Glace

		4th	5th	6th	7th	8th	9th
To fit		2-3	3-4	4-5	6-7	8-9	9-10 yrs
Chest size		22	23	24	26	28	30in
		(56	58	61	66	71	76cm)
A Cndy Fl	747	4	5	5	6	7	8 x 50gm
B Bubbles	724	2	2	2	2	2	3 x 50gm
C Butter	795	1	1	1	1	1	1 x 50gm

NEEDLES

1 pair 2¾mm (no 12) (US 2) needles
1 pair 3¼mm (no 10) (US 3) needles

BUTTONS

5

TENSION

23 sts and 32 rows to 10 cm measured over
patterned stocking stitch using 3¼mm (US 3)
needles.

BACK

Cast on 67 (71: 77: 83: 93: 97) sts using 2¾mm
(US 2) needles and yarn A.
Knit 3 rows.
Row 4 (WS): K0 (0: 1: 0: 1: 1), *P1, K1, rep
from * to last 1 (1: 0: 1: 0: 0) st, P1 (1: 0: 1: 0: 0).
Row 5: As row 4.
Last 2 rows form moss st.
Work a further 3 rows in moss st.
Change to 3¼mm (US 3) needles.
Using the **intarsia** technique described on the
information page, starting and ending rows as
indicated, and beg with a K row, work in patt
from chart for back, which is worked mainly in
st st, as folls:
Cont in patt foll chart, inc 1 st at each end of chart
row 9 (9: 9: 7: 7: 5) and every foll 16th (16th: 16th:
14th: 14th: 12th) row until there are 71 (75: 81:
89: 99: 105) sts, taking inc sts into patt.
Cont straight until chart row 44 (48: 50: 56: 62: 66)
has been completed, ending with a WS row.
Shape armholes
Keeping chart correct, cast off 3 (3: 3: 4: 4: 4) sts
at beg of next 2 rows. 65 (69: 75: 81: 91: 97) sts.
Dec 1 st at each end of next 3 rows.
59 (63: 69: 75: 85: 91) sts.

Cont straight until chart row 94 (100: 106: 114:
122: 130) has been completed, ending with a
WS row.
Shape shoulders and back neck
Cast off 6 (6: 7: 7: 9: 9) sts at beg of next 2 rows.
47 (51: 55: 61: 67: 73) sts.
Next row (RS): Cast off 6 (6: 7: 7: 9: 9) sts, patt
until there are 9 (10: 10: 12: 12: 14) sts on right
needle and turn, leaving rem sts on a holder.
Work each side of neck separately.
Cast off 4 sts at beg of next row.
Cast off rem 5 (6: 6: 8: 8: 10) sts.
With RS facing, rejoin yarn to rem sts, cast off
centre 17 (19: 21: 23: 25: 27) sts, patt to end.
Work to match first side, reversing shapings.

LEFT FRONT

Cast on 39 (41: 44: 47: 52: 54) sts using 2¾mm
(US 2) needles and yarn A.
Knit 3 rows.
Row 4 (WS): *P1, K1, rep from * to last 1 (1: 0:
1: 0: 0) st, P1 (1: 0: 1: 0: 0).
Row 5: P1 (1: 0: 1: 0: 0), *K1, P1, rep from * to
end.
Last 2 rows form moss st.
Work a further 3 rows in moss st.
Change to 3¼mm (US 3) needles.
Work in patt from chart for front as folls:
Cont in patt foll chart, inc 1 st at beg of chart
row 9 (9: 9: 7: 7: 5) and every foll 16th (16th: 16th:
14th: 14th: 12th) row until there are 41 (43: 46:
50: 55: 58) sts, taking inc sts into patt.
Cont straight until chart row 44 (48: 50: 56: 62: 66)
has been completed, ending with a WS row.
Shape armhole
Keeping chart correct, cast off 3 (3: 3: 4: 4: 4) sts
at beg of next row.
38 (40: 43: 46: 51: 54) sts.
Work 1 row.
Dec 1 st at armhole edge of next 3 rows.
35 (37: 40: 43: 48: 51) sts.
Cont straight until chart row 82 (86: 90: 96: 102:
108) has been completed, ending with a WS
row.
Shape neck
Next row (RS): Patt to last 12 sts and turn,
leaving last 12 sts on a holder.
23 (25: 28: 31: 36: 39) sts.
Dec 1 st at neck edge of next 3 rows, then on
every foll alt row until 17 (18: 20: 22: 26: 28) sts
rem.
Cont straight until chart row 94 (100: 106: 114:
122: 130) has been completed, ending with a
WS row.
Shape shoulder
Cast off 6 (6: 7: 7: 9: 9) sts at beg of next and foll
alt row.
Work 1 row.
Cast off rem 5 (6: 6: 8: 8: 10) sts.

RIGHT FRONT

Cast on 39 (41: 44: 47: 52: 54) sts using 2¾mm
(US 2) needles and yarn A.
Knit 3 rows.
Row 4 (WS): P1 (1: 0: 1: 0: 0), *K1, P1, rep
from * to end.
Row 5: P1, K1, P1, cast off 2 sts (one st on right
needle after cast-off), *P1, K1, rep from * to last
1 (1: 0: 1: 0: 0) st, P1 (1: 0: 1: 0: 0).
Last 2 rows form moss st.
Rows 6: Moss st to end, casting on 2 sts over
those cast off on previous row.
Work a further 2 rows in moss st.
Change to 3¼mm (US 3) needles.
Work in patt from chart for front as folls:

Making a further 4 buttonholes in every foll
20th (22nd: 22nd: 24th: 26th: 26th) row from
previous buttonhole, cont as folls:
Cont in patt foll chart, inc 1 st at end of chart
row 9 (9: 9: 7: 7: 5) and every foll 16th (16th:
16th: 14th: 14th: 12th) row until there are
41 (43: 46: 50: 55: 58) sts, taking inc sts into patt.
Cont straight until chart row 45 (49: 51: 57: 63: 67)
has been completed, ending with a RS row.
Shape armhole
Keeping chart correct, cast off 3 (3: 3: 4: 4: 4) sts
at beg of next row.
38 (40: 43: 46: 51: 54) sts.
Dec 1 st at armhole edge of next 3 rows.
35 (37: 40: 43: 48: 51) sts.
Cont straight until chart row 82 (86: 90: 96: 102:
108) has been completed, ending with a WS
row.
Shape neck
Next row (RS): Cast off 5 sts, patt until there
are 7 sts on right needle and slip these sts onto a
holder, patt to end.
23 (25: 28: 31: 36: 39) sts.
Dec 1 st at neck edge of next 3 rows, then on
every foll alt row until 17 (18: 20: 22: 26: 28) sts
rem.
Cont straight until chart row 95 (101: 107: 115:
123: 131) has been completed, ending with a RS
row.
Shape shoulder
Cast off 6 (6: 7: 7: 9: 9) sts at beg of next and foll
alt row.
Work 1 row.
Cast off rem 5 (6: 6: 8: 8: 10) sts.

SLEEVES (both alike)

Cast on 37 (37: 41: 41: 45: 45) sts using 2¾mm
(US 2) needles and yarn A.
Knit 3 rows.
Row 4 (WS): K0 (0: 1: 0: 1: 1), *P1, K1, rep
from * to last 1 (1: 0: 1: 0: 0) st, P1 (1: 0: 1: 0: 0).
Row 5: As row 4.
Last 2 rows form moss st.
Work a further 3 rows in moss st, inc 1 st at each
end of 2nd of these rows.
39 (39: 43: 43: 47: 47) sts.
Change to 3¼mm (US 3) needles.
Noting that sleeves are only shown on chart to
row 40 and thereafter referring back to motifs
below row 40 as markers and working incs and
sleevehead from instructions, work in patt from
chart for sleeve as folls:
Cont in patt foll chart, inc 1 st at each end of
chart row 3 and every foll 4th row until there
are 69 (73: 75: 75: 77: 77) sts, taking inc sts into
patt.
6th, 7th, 8th and 9th sizes only
Inc 1 st at each end of every foll 6th row until
there are – (–: 79: 83: 87: 93) sts.
All sizes
Cont straight until chart row 68 (76: 86: 100:
110: 122) has been completed, ending with a
WS row.
Shape top
Keeping chart correct, cast off 3 (3: 3: 4: 4: 4) sts
at beg of next 2 rows.
63 (67: 73: 75: 79: 85) sts.
Dec 1 st at each end of next and foll 2 alt rows.
Work 1 row.
Cast off rem 57 (61: 67: 69: 73: 79) sts.

MAKING UP

PRESS all pieces as described on the
information page.
Join shoulder seams using back stitch.

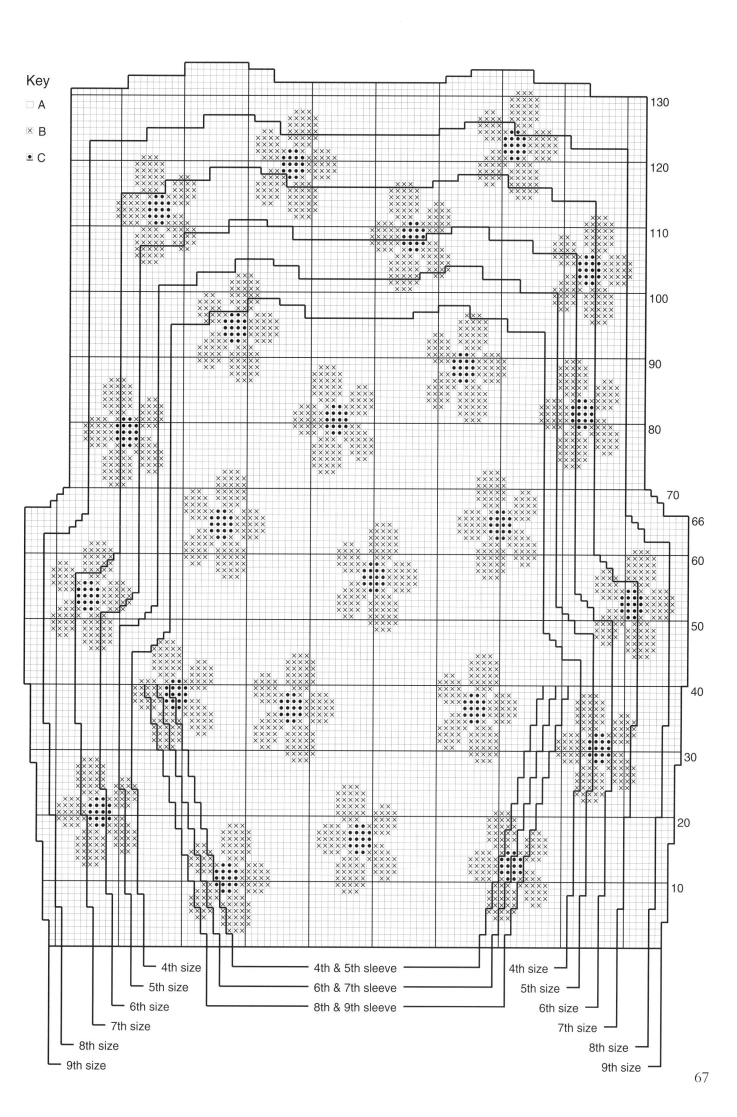

Key

☐ A

☒ B

⚈ C

130

120

110

100

90

80

70

66

60

50

40

30

20

10

—— 4th size ——

—— 5th size ——

—— 6th size ——

—— 7th size ——

—— 8th size ——

—— 9th size ——

—— 4th & 5th sleeve ——

—— 6th & 7th sleeve ——

—— 8th & 9th sleeve ——

—— 4th size ——

—— 5th size ——

—— 6th size ——

—— 7th size ——

—— 8th size ——

—— 9th size ——

67

Neck border

With RS facing, yarn A and 2¾mm (US 2) needles, slip 7 sts from right front holder onto RH needle, rejoin yarn and pick up and knit

15 (17: 19: 21: 23: 25) sts up right side of neck, 25 (27: 29: 31: 33: 35) sts from back neck, 15 (17: 19: 21: 23: 25) sts down left side of neck, then patt across 12 sts from left front holder. 74 (80: 86: 92: 98: 104) sts.
Keeping moss st correct as set by front opening borders, cont as folls:
Cast off 5 sts at beg of next row.
69 (75: 81: 87: 93: 99) sts.
Work 4 rows in moss st.

Knit 3 rows.
Cast off knitwise (on WS).
See information page for finishing instructions, setting in sleeves using the shallow set-in method.

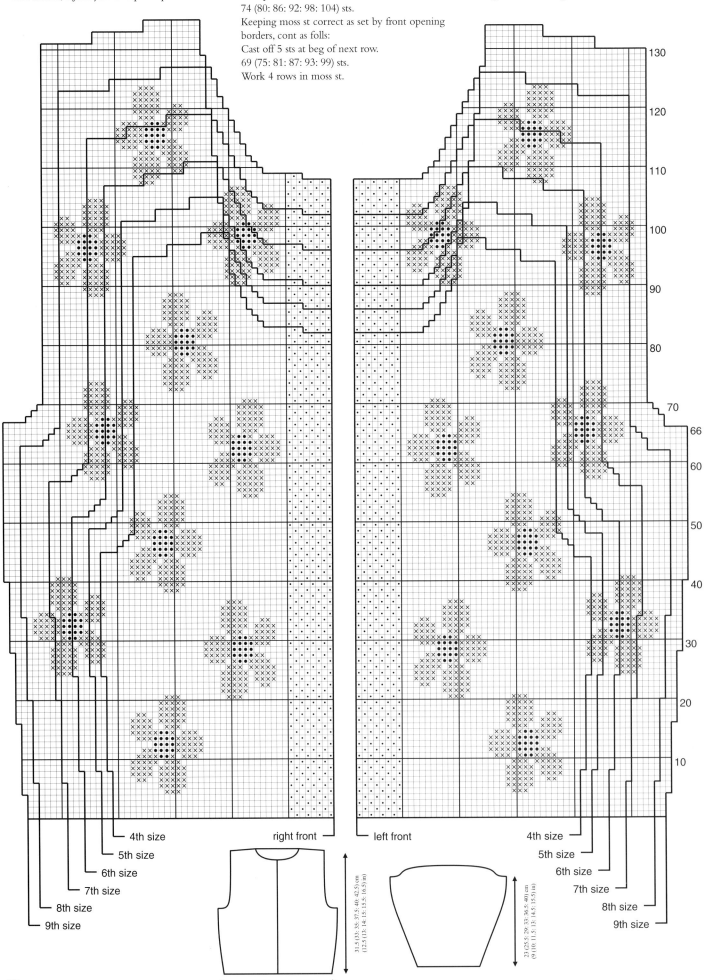

right front — left front

4th size
5th size
6th size
7th size
8th size
9th size

4th size
5th size
6th size
7th size
8th size
9th size

31.5 (33: 35: 37.5: 40: 42.5) cm
(12.5 (13: 14: 15: 15.5: 16.5) in)

23 (25.5: 29: 33: 36.5: 40) cm
(9 (10: 11.5: 13: 14.5: 15.5) in)

31 (32.5: 35: 38.5: 43: 45.5) cm
(12 (13: 14: 15: 17: 18) in)

Mimi

YARN

Rowan 4 ply Cotton

	1st	2nd	
To fit	0–6	6–12	mths
Chest size	16	18	in
	(41	46	cm)
	3	3	x 50 gm

3rd	4th	5th	6th	7th	8th	9th		
To fit								
1–2	2–3	3–4	4–5	6–7	8–9	9–10		yrs
Chest size								
20	22	23	24	26	28	30		in
(51	56	58	61	66	71	76		cm)
4	4	5	6	7	8	8		x 50 gm

(photographed in Bleached 113 and Allure 119)

NEEDLES

1 pair 2¼mm (no 13) (US 1) needles
1 pair 2¾mm (no 12) (US 2) needles

BUTTONS

5 (5: 5: 5: 5: 6: 6: 6: 6)

TENSION

30 sts and 50 rows to 10 cm measured over moss st using 2¾mm (US 2) needles.

Pattern note: As row end edges of fronts form actual finished edges of garment, it is important that these edges are kept neat. Therefore, all new balls of yarn should be joined in at side seam or armhole edges of rows.

BACK

Cast on 147 (159: 159: 171: 183: 201: 219: 243: 255) sts using 2¼mm (US 1) needles and work edging as folls:
Row 1 (RS)(dec): K3, ★cast off 3 sts, K3, rep from ★ to end.
75 (81: 81: 87: 93: 102: 111: 123: 129) sts.
Work 3 rows in garter st, ending with a WS row, dec 0 (0: 0: 2: 0: 1: 2: 2: 2) sts at end(s) of last row.
75 (81: 81: 85: 93: 101: 109: 121: 127) sts.
Change to 2¾mm (US 2) needles and knit 1 row.
Next row (WS): K1, ★P1, K1, rep from ★ to end.
Next row: As last row.
These 2 rows form moss st and are rep throughout.
1st and 2nd sizes only
Cont straight until back measures 11.5 (13) cm from cast-on edge, ending with a WS row.
Shape armholes
Keeping patt correct, cast off 6 sts at beg of next 2 rows. 63 (69) sts.
3rd, 4th, 5th, 6th, 7th, 8th and 9th sizes only
Keeping patt correct, inc 1 st at each end of 11th and every foll – (–: 14th: 14th: 14th: 14th: 14th: 16th: 16th) row until there are – (–: 87: 91: 99: 107: 117: 129: 137) sts.
Cont straight until back measures – (–: 16.5: 16.5: 17: 18.5: 20: 22: 23) cm from cast-on edge, ending with a WS row.
Shape armholes
Cast off 4 sts at beg of next 2 rows.
– (–:79: 83: 91: 99: 109: 121: 129) sts.
Keeping patt correct, cont to shape armhole by dec 1 st each end of every row until – (–: 75: 75: 83: 91: 99: 111: 119) sts rem.
All sizes
Cont straight until armhole measures 11.5 (12.5: 14: 15: 16: 17: 18: 19: 20) cm, ending with a WS row.
Shape shoulders and back neck
Cast off 5 (6: 7: 7: 8: 9: 10: 11: 12) sts at beg of next 2 rows.
53 (57: 61: 61: 67: 73: 79: 89: 95) sts.
Next row (RS): Cast off 5 (6: 7: 7: 8: 9: 10: 11: 12) sts, patt until there are 10 (11: 11: 11: 11: 13: 14: 16: 17) sts on right needle and turn, leaving rem sts on a holder.
Work each side of neck separately.
Cast off 4 sts at beg of next row.
Cast off rem 6 (7: 7: 7: 7: 9: 10: 12: 13) sts.
With RS facing, rejoin yarn to rem sts, cast off centre 23 (23: 25: 25: 29: 29: 31: 35: 37) sts, patt to end.
Work to match first side, reversing shaping.

LEFT FRONT

Cast on 81 (87: 87: 93: 99: 111: 117: 129: 135) sts using 2¼mm (US 1) needles and work edging as folls:
Row 1 (RS)(dec): K3, ★cast off 3 sts, K3, rep from ★ to end. 42 (45: 45: 48: 51: 57: 60: 66: 69) sts.
Work 3 rows in garter st, ending with a WS row, dec 1 (1: 1: 2: 0: 2: 1: 1: 1) sts at end(s) of last row. 41 (44: 44: 46: 51: 55: 59: 65: 68) sts.
Change to 2¾mm (US 2) needles and knit 1 row.
1st and 2nd sizes only
Cont in moss st as given for back until left front matches back to beg of armhole shaping, ending with a WS row.
Shape armhole
Keeping patt correct, cast off 6 sts at beg of next row. 35 (38) sts.
3rd, 4th, 5th, 6th, 7th, 8th and 9th sizes only
Cont in moss st as given for back, inc 1 st at beg of 11th and every foll – (–: 14th: 14th: 14th: 14th: 14th: 16th: 16th) row until there are – (–: 47: 49: 54: 58: 63: 69: 73) sts.
Cont straight until left front matches back to beg of armhole shaping, ending with a WS row.
Shape armholes
Cast off 4 sts at beg of next row.
– (–: 43: 45: 50: 54: 59: 65: 69) sts.
Work 1 row.
Keeping patt correct, dec 1 st armhole edge of every row until – (–: 41: 41: 46: 50: 54: 60: 64) sts rem.
All sizes
Cont straight until left front is 13 (13: 15: 15: 21: 21: 23: 25: 29) rows shorter than back to start of shoulder shaping, ending with a RS row.
Shape neck
Next row (WS): Cast off 11 (11: 12: 12: 13: 13: 14: 14: 15) sts at beg of next row.
24 (27: 29: 29: 33: 37: 40: 46: 49) sts.
Next row (RS)(dec): Moss st to last 5 sts, patt 3 tog, moss st to end.
Work 1 row.
Cont in moss st, dec as before on next and foll 1 (1: 1: 1: 1: 1: 1: 2: 1) alt rows, then on every foll 4th row until 16 (19: 21: 21: 23: 27: 30: 34: 37) sts rem.
Work straight until left front matches back to start of shoulder shaping, ending with a WS row.
Shape shoulder
Cast off 5 (6: 7: 7: 8: 9: 10: 11: 12) sts at beg of next and foll alt row.
Work 1 row.
Cast off rem 6 (7: 7: 7: 7: 9: 10: 12: 13) sts.
Mark the positions of 5 (5: 5: 5: 5: 6: 6: 6: 6) buttons, the first to come 2.5 cm from cast-on edge, the last one 1.5 cm down from neck edge and rem buttons spaced evenly between.

RIGHT FRONT

Cast on 81 (87: 87: 93: 99: 111: 117: 129: 135) sts using 2¼mm (US 1) needles and work edging as folls:
Row 1 (RS)(dec): K3, ★cast off 3 sts, K3, rep from ★ to end.
42 (45: 45: 48: 51: 57: 60: 66: 69) sts.
Work 3 rows in garter st, ending with a WS row, dec 1 (1: 1: 2: 0: 2: 1: 1: 1) sts at end(s) of last row.
41 (44: 44: 46: 51: 55: 59: 65: 68) sts.
Change to 2¾mm (US 2) needles and knit 1 row.
Cont in moss st, complete to match left front, reversing all shaping, and with the addition of 5 (5: 5: 5: 5: 6: 6: 6: 6) buttonholes to correspond with positions marked for buttons, worked as folls:
Next row (buttonhole row)(RS): Moss st 3 (3: 3: 3: 4: 4: 4: 4: 4), yrn, work 2 tog, moss st to end.

SLEEVES (both alike)

Cast on 75 (87: 87: 99: 99: 105: 111: 111: 123) sts using 2¼mm (US 1) needles and work edging as folls:
Row 1 (RS)(dec): K3, ★cast off 3 sts, K3, rep from ★ to end.
39 (45: 45: 51: 51: 54: 57: 57: 63) sts.
Work 3 rows in garter st, ending with a WS row, dec 2 (2: 0: 2: 0: 1: 2: 0: 2) sts at end(s) of last row.
37 (43: 45: 49: 51: 53: 55: 57: 61) sts.
Change to 2¾mm (US 2) needles.

Cont in moss st as given for back, shaping sleeve seam by inc 1 st at each end of 7th and every foll 4th (6th: 6th: 6th: 6th: 6th: 6th: 6th: 6th) row to 55 (53: 49: 69: 75: 77: 91: 97: 121) sts, then on every foll alt (4th: 4th: 4th: 4th: 4th: 4th: 4th: 0) row to 69 (75: 85: 91: 97: 103: 109: 115: 121) sts. Cont without further shaping until sleeve measures 14.5 (18.5: 18: 24: 26.5: 29.5: 33.5: 37: 40.5) cm from cast-on edge, ending with a WS row.

1st and 2nd sizes only
Cast off loosely and evenly.

3rd, 4th, 5th, 6th, 7th, 8th and 9th sizes only
Shape top
Keeping moss st correct, cast off 4 sts at beg of next 2 rows. – (–: 77: 83: 89: 95: 101: 107: 113) sts. Cont in patt, dec 1 st at each end of next and foll – (–: 1: 3: 3: 3: 4: 4: 4) alt rows.
– (–: 73: 75: 81: 87: 91: 97: 103) sts.
Work 1 row. Cast off evenly.

MAKING UP
PRESS all pieces as described on the info page. Join both shoulder seams using back stitch. Set sleeve into armhole using the shallow set-in method described on the information page. Sew on buttons to correspond with buttonholes. See information page for finishing instructions.

Design number 20

Harry

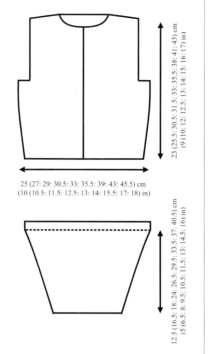

YARN
Rowan All Seasons Cotton

	3rd	4th	5th	6th	7th	8th	9th	
To fit								
1-2	2-3	3-4	4-5	6-7	8-9	9-10 yrs		
Chest size								
20	22	23	24	26	28	30	in	
(51	56	58	61	66	71	76	cm)	
5	6	7	8	9	11	13	x 50gm	

(photographed in Iceberg 192)

NEEDLES
1 pair 4mm (no 8) (US 6) needles
1 pair 4½mm (no 7) (US 7) needles
1 pair 5mm (no 6) (US 8) needles

TENSION
17 sts and 24 rows to 10 cm measured over stocking stitch using 5mm (US 8) needles.

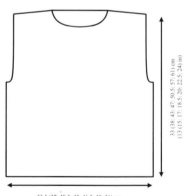

23 (25.5: 30.5: 31.5: 33: 35.5: 38: 41: 43) cm
(9 (10: 12: 12.5: 13: 14: 15: 16: 17) in)

25 (27: 29: 30.5: 33: 35.5: 39: 43: 45.5) cm
(10 (10.5: 11.5: 12.5: 13: 14: 15.5: 17: 18) in)

12.5 (16.5: 18: 24: 26.5: 29.5: 33.5: 37: 40.5) cm
(5 (6.5: 8: 9.5: 10.5: 11.5: 13: 14.5: 16) in)

BACK
Cast on 57 (63: 69: 73: 79: 85: 95) sts using 4mm (US 6) needles.
Row 1 (RS): P0 (0: 0: 0: 2: 0: 0), K0 (3: 0: 2: 3: 2: 1), ★P3, K3, rep from ★ to last 3 (0: 3: 5: 2: 5: 4) sts, P3 (0: 3: 2: 3: 3) , K0 (0: 0: 2: 0: 2: 1).
Row 2: K0 (0: 0: 0: 2: 0: 0), P0 (3: 0: 2: 3: 2: 1), ★K3, P3, rep from ★ to last 3 (0: 3: 5: 2: 5: 4) sts, K3 (0: 3: 2: 3: 3), P0 (0: 0: 2: 0: 2: 1).
Rep these 2 rows 5 (5: 5: 6: 6: 6: 6) times more.
Change to 5mm (US 8) needles.
Beg with a K row, work in st st until back measures 18 (21.5: 25.5: 28: 30.5: 35.5: 38) cm from cast-on edge, ending with a WS row.
Shape armholes
Cast off 4 (4: 4: 4: 5: 5: 5) sts at beg of next 2 rows.
49 (55: 61: 65: 69: 75: 85) sts.
Cont straight until armhole measures 15 (16.5: 17.5: 19: 20: 21.5: 23) cm, ending with a WS row.
Shape shoulders and back neck
Cast off 4 (5: 6: 6: 7: 8: 9) sts at beg of next 2 rows.
41 (45: 49: 53: 55: 59: 67) sts.
Next row (RS): Cast off 4 (5: 6: 6: 7: 8: 9) sts, K until there are 9 (9: 10: 11: 11: 11: 13) sts on right needle and turn, leaving rem sts on a holder.
Work each side of neck separately.
Cast off 4 sts at beg of next row.
Cast off rem 5 (5: 6: 7: 7: 7: 9) sts.
With RS facing, rejoin yarn to rem sts, cast off centre 15 (17: 17: 19: 19: 21: 23) sts, K to end.
Work to match first side, reversing shapings.

FRONT
Work as for back until 10 (10: 12: 12: 14: 14: 16) rows less have been worked than on back to start of shoulder shaping, ending with a WS row.
Shape neck
Next row (RS): K18 (20: 23: 24: 27: 29: 33) and turn, leaving rem sts on a holder.
Work each side of neck separately.
Dec 1 st at neck edge of next 4 rows, then on foll 1 (1: 1: 1: 2: 2: 2) alt rows.
13 (15: 18: 19: 21: 23: 27) sts.
Work 3 (3: 5: 5: 5: 5: 7) rows.

Shape shoulder
Cast off 4 (5: 6: 6: 7: 8: 9) sts at beg of next and foll alt row.
Work 1 row. Cast off rem 5 (5: 6: 7: 7: 7: 9) sts.
With RS facing, rejoin yarn to rem sts, cast off centre 13 (15: 15: 17: 15: 17: 19) sts, K to end.
Work to match first side, reversing shapings.

SLEEVES (both alike)
Cast on 31 (33: 35: 37: 39: 41: 43) sts using 4mm (US 6) needles.
Row 1 (RS): P0 (0: 1: 2: 0: 0: 0), K2 (3: 3: 3: 0: 1: 2), ★P3, K3, rep from ★ to last 5 (0: 1: 2: 3: 4: 5) sts, P3 (0: 1: 2: 3: 3: 3), K2 (0: 0: 0: 0: 1: 2).
Row 2: K0 (0: 1: 2: 0: 0: 0), P2 (3: 3: 3: 0: 1: 2), ★K3, P3, rep from ★ to last 5 (0: 1: 2: 3: 4: 5) sts, K3 (0: 1: 2: 3: 3: 3), P2 (0: 0: 0: 0: 1: 2).
These 2 rows form K3, P3 rib.
Keeping rib correct as set, proceed as folls:
Work a further 14 rows.
Change to 5mm (US 8) needles and cont in rib, inc 1 st at each end of 3rd and every foll 4th (4th: 4th: 4th: 6th: 6th: 6th) row to 43 (49: 53: 59: 43: 47: 47) sts, then on every foll alt (alt: alt: alt: 4th: 4th: 4th) row until there are 51 (57: 61: 65: 69: 73: 79) sts, taking inc sts into rib.
Cont straight until sleeve measures 25.5 (29: 30.5: 33.5: 38.5: 41: 43.5) cm from cast-on edge, ending with a WS row.
Cast off loosely in rib.

MAKING UP
PRESS all pieces as described on the info page. Join right shoulder seam using back stitch.
Neck border
With RS facing and 4½mm (US 7) needles, pick up and knit 12 (13: 13: 14: 15: 16: 17) sts down left front neck, 13 (15: 15: 17: 15: 17: 19) sts across front neck, 12 (13: 13: 14: 15: 16: 17) sts up right front neck, and 23 (25: 25: 27: 27: 29: 31) sts across back neck. 60 (66: 66: 72: 72: 78: 84) sts.
Next row: ★K3, P3, rep from ★ to end.
Rep last row for 6 (6: 6: 7.5: 7.5: 7.5: 7.5) cm.
Cast off loosely in rib.
Join left shoulder and neck border seam using back stitch. Set sleeves into armholes using the square set-in method described on the information page. See information page for finishing instructions. Fold 5 cm cuff to RS.

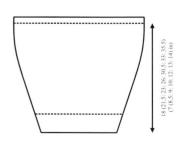

33 (38: 43: 47: 50.5: 57: 61) cm
(13 (15: 17: 18.5: 20: 22.5: 24) in)

33.5 (37: 40.5: 43: 46.5: 50: 56) cm
(13 (14.5: 16: 17: 18.5: 19.5: 22) in)

18 (21.5: 23: 26: 30.5: 33: 35.5)
(7 (8.5: 9: 10: 12: 13: 14) in)

Design number 21

Strawberry

YARN
Rowan 4-ply Botany

		1st	2nd	3rd	4th		
To fit		0-6	6-12m	1-2	2-3 yrs		
Chest size		16	18	20	22	in	
		(41	46	51	56	cm)	
A Fr. Green	573	1	1	1	1	x	50gm
B Lavender	571	1	1	1	1	x	50gm
C Oxford	574	1	1	1	1	x	50gm
D Bay	575	1	1	1	1	x	50gm
E Frost	552	1	1	1	1	x	50gm
F Redwood	549	1	1	1	1	x	50gm
G Strwberry	560	1	1	1	2	x	50gm

NEEDLES
1 pair 2¾mm (no 12) (US 2) needles
1 pair 3¼mm (no 10) (US 3) needles

BUTTONS
5 (5: 6: 6)

TENSION
28 sts and 36 rows to 10 cm measured over stocking stitch using 3¼mm (US 3) needles.

BODY (worked in one piece to armholes)
Cast on 139 (164: 184: 209) sts using 2¾mm (US 2) needles and yarn A.
Starting and ending rows as indicated and beg with a K row, cont in patt from chart, which is worked entirely in st st, using the **fairisle** technique described on the information page for the heart and flower motifs.
Work 8 rows.
Change to 3¼mm (US 3) needles.
Cont straight until work measures 13 (16.5: 19.5: 23) cm from cast-on edge, ending with a WS row.
Divide for armholes
Next row (RS): Patt 30 (37: 41: 48) sts and slip these sts onto a holder for right front, cast off 9 sts, patt until there are 61 (72: 84: 95) sts on right needle, turn and leave rem 39 (46: 50: 57) sts on a second holder for left front.
Shape back
Cont in patt on centre 61 (72: 84: 95) sts until armhole measures 11.5 (13: 15: 16.5) cm, ending with a WS row.

Shape shoulders and back neck
Cast off 5 (6: 8: 9) sts at beg of next 2 rows.
51 (60: 68: 77) sts.
Next row (RS): Cast off 5 (6: 8: 9) sts, patt until there are 9 (11: 12: 14) sts on right needle and turn, leaving rem sts on a holder.
Work each side of neck separately.
Cast off 4 sts at beg of next row.
Cast off rem 5 (7: 8: 10) sts.
With RS facing, rejoin yarn to rem sts, cast off centre 23 (26: 28: 31) sts, patt to end.
Work to match first side, reversing shapings.
Shape left front
Return to sts left on second st holder, rejoin yarn with RS facing, cast off 9 sts, patt to end.
30 (37: 41: 48) sts
Cont straight until 9 (11: 13: 13) rows less have been worked than on back to start of shoulder shaping, ending with a RS row.
Shape neck
Keeping patt correct, cast off 11 (13: 11: 14) sts at beg of next row. 19 (24: 30: 34) sts.
Dec 1 st at neck edge of next 3 rows, then on every foll alt row until 15 (19: 24: 28) sts rem.
Work 3 rows, ending with a WS row.
Shape shoulder
Cast off 5 (6: 8: 9) sts at beg of next and foll alt row.
Work 1 row. Cast off rem 5 (7: 8: 10) sts.
Shape right front
Return to sts left on first st holder, rejoin yarn with WS facing and patt to end. 30 (37: 41: 48) sts
Complete to match left front, reversing shapings.

SLEEVES (both alike)
Cast on 42 (47: 51: 56) sts using 2¾mm (US 2) needles and yarn A.
Starting and ending rows as indicated and beg with a K row, work in patt from chart as folls:
Work 8 rows.
Change to 3¼mm (US 3) needles.
Cont in patt as set, inc 1 st at each end of next and every foll 4th row to 52 (69: 71: 84) sts, then on every foll alt row until there are 66 (73: 85: 94) sts, taking inc sts into patt. (Note: chart only shows incs for first 35 rows. After this, position flowers and hearts directly above first band of hearts.)
Cont straight until work measures 14.5 (18.5: 20: 23.5) cm from cast-on edge, ending with a WS row.
Cast off.

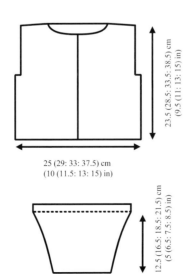

23.5 (28.5: 33.5: 38.5) cm
(9.5 (11: 13: 15) in)

25 (29: 33: 37.5) cm
(10 (11.5: 13: 15) in)

12.5 (16.5: 18.5: 21.5) cm
(5 (6.5: 7.5: 8.5) in)

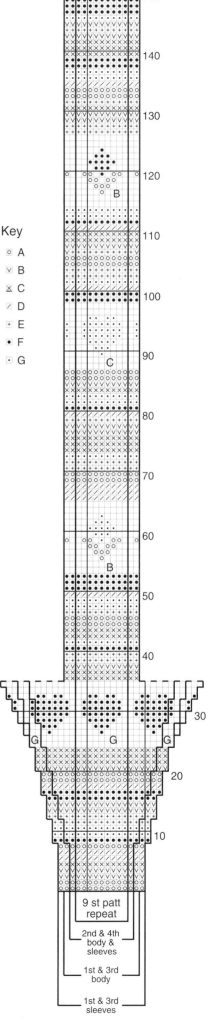

Key
- ⊙ A
- ⊻ B
- ⊠ C
- ⊿ D
- + E
- • F
- ⸳ G

9 st patt repeat

2nd & 4th body & sleeves

1st & 3rd body

1st & 3rd sleeves

MAKING UP

PRESS all pieces as described on the info page. Join shoulder seams using back stitch.

Button border

With RS facing, yarn B and 2¾mm (US 2) needles, pick up and knit 59 (71: 87: 102) sts along left front opening edge, between beg of first row in yarn B and neck shaping.

Beg with a K row, work 4 rows in st st.

Cast off knitwise (on WS).

Buttonhole border

Work as for button border with the addition of 5 (5: 6: 6) buttonholes in 2nd row worked as folls:

Next row (buttonhole row) (RS): P3, *yrn, P2tog, P11 (14: 14: 17), rep from * to last 4 sts, yrn, P2tog, P2.

Neck border

With RS facing, yarn B and 2¾mm (US 2) needles, starting and ending halfway across top of borders, pick up and knit 21 (24: 25: 27) sts up right side of neck, 31 (34: 36: 39) sts from back neck, and 21 (24: 25: 27) sts down left side of neck. 73 (82: 86: 93) sts.

Beg with a K row, work 4 rows in st st.

Cast off knitwise (on WS).

See information page for finishing instructions, setting in sleeves using the square set-in method and allowing 1 cm at cast-on edges of sleeves and body to rollout to RS.

Design number 22

Cheesecake bag

YARN

Rowan Cotton Glace

A	Bubbles	724	1	x	50gm
B	Terracotta	786	1	x	50gm
C	Mint	748	1	x	50gm
D	Hyacinth	787	1	x	50gm
E	Candy Floss	747	1	x	50gm
F	Blood Orange	445	1	x	50gm
G	Pear	780	1	x	50gm
H	Butter	795	1	x	50gm

NEEDLES

1 pair 2¾mm (no 12) (US 2) needles
1 pair 3¼mm (no 10) (US 3) needles

TENSION

23 sts and 32 rows to 10 cm measured over patterned st st using 3¼mm (US 3) needles.

MEASUREMENTS

Finished bag is approx 24 cm (9½ in) wide and 28 cm (11 in) deep.

SIDES (both alike)

Cast on 55 sts using 3¼mm (US 3) needles and yarn A.

Using the **fairisle** technique described on the information page, work 87 rows in patt from chart, which is worked entirely in st st, beg with a K row. Break off all contrast colours and complete using yarn A as folls:

Purl 1 row.

Next row (eyelet row)(RS): K2, *yfwd, K2tog, K5, rep from * to last 4 sts, yfwd, K2tog, K2.

Change to 2¾mm (US 2) needles and work 4 rows in garter st, ending with a RS row.

Cast off evenly knitwise (on WS).

CORD GUIDES (make 2)

Cast on 4 sts using 2¾mm (US 2) needles and yarn A.

Row 1 (RS): K1, P2, K1.

Row 2: K4.

Work a further 14 rows in rev st st as set. Cast off.

With WS together, fold each cord guide in half and catch tog at base.

MAKING UP

Press all pieces as described on the info page.

With right sides facing, sew pieces together along side and lower edges using back stitch, inserting one cord guide at base of each side seam. Leave cast-off edges open. Turn right side out.

Using 3 strands of yarn A, make 2 twisted cords, each approx 100 cm long. Using photograph as a guide, take one cord and thread it through the cord guide, in and out of the eyelets along one side of opening edge and down through opposite cord guide. Repeat using second cord and opposite opening edge of bag, knotting ends of cords tog at base of bag.

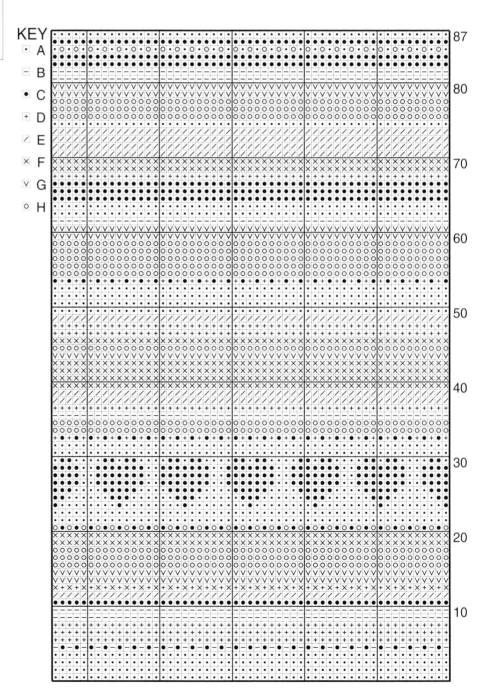

Design number 23

Lucky

YARN
Rowan All Seasons Cotton

	1st	2nd	3rd	
To fit	0-6 mths	6-12 mths	1-2 yrs	
Chest size	16	18	20	in
	(41	46	51	cm)
	3	3	4	x 50gm

(photographed in Limedrop 197)

NEEDLES
1 pair 4mm (no 8) (US 6) needles
1 pair 5 mm (no 6) (US 8) needles

BUTTONS – 1

TENSION
18 sts and 30 rows to 10 cm measured over moss st using 5 mm (US 8) needles.

Pattern note: As row end edges of fronts form actual finished edges of garment, it is important that these edges are kept neat. Therefore, all new balls of yarn should be joined in at side seam or armhole edges of rows.

BACK
Cast on 45 (49: 53) sts using 4mm (US 6) needles.
Work 3 rows in garter st, ending with a RS row.
Change to 5 mm (US 8) needles and work in moss st as folls:
Next row (WS): P1, *K1, P1, rep from * to end.
Next row: As last row.
Cont in moss st as set until work measures 11.5 (12.5: 16.5) cm from cast-on edge, ending with a WS row.
Shape armholes
Cast off 4 sts at beg of next 2 rows. 37 (41: 45) sts.
Cont straight until armhole measures 11.5 (12.5: 14) cm, ending with a WS row.
Shape shoulders and back neck
Cast off 5 (6: 6) sts at beg of next 2 rows and 5 (6: 7) sts at beg of foll 2 rows.
Cast off rem 17 (17: 19) sts.

LEFT FRONT
Cast on 26 (28: 31) sts using 4mm (US 6) needles.
Work 3 rows in garter st, ending with a RS row.

Change to 5 mm (US 8) needles and work in moss st as folls:
Next row (WS): P0 (0: 1), *K1, P1, rep from * to end.
Next row: *P1, K1, rep from * to last 0 (0: 1) st, P0 (0: 1).
Cont in moss st until left front matches back to beg of armhole shaping, ending with a WS row.
Shape armhole
Cast off 4 sts at beg of next row. 22 (24: 27) sts.
Cont straight until left front is 16 (16: 18) rows shorter than back to start of shoulder shaping, ending with a WS row.
Shape neck
Next row (RS): Moss st to last 5 sts, patt 3 tog, moss st 2. 20 (22: 25) sts.
Work 1 row.
Dec 2 sts as before on next and every foll alt row until 10 (12: 13) sts rem.
Work 5 rows, ending with a WS row.
Shape shoulder
Cast off 5 (6: 6) sts at beg of next row.
Work 1 row.
Cast off rem 5 (6: 7) sts.

RIGHT FRONT
Cast on 26 (28: 31) sts using 4mm (US 6) needles.
Work 3 rows in garter st, ending with a RS row.
Change to 5 mm (US 8) needles and work in moss st as folls:
Next row (WS): *P1, K1, rep from * to last 0 (0: 1) st, P0 (0: 1).
Next row: P0 (0: 1), *K1, P1, rep from * to end.
Cont as for left front, reversing shapings, until 20 (20: 22) rows less have been worked than on back to **start** of shoulder shaping, ending with a WS row.
Next row (RS)(buttonhole row): Moss st 3 (3: 4), cast off 2 sts, moss st to end.
Next row: Moss st to end, casting on 2 sts over those cast off on previous row.
Complete to match left front, reversing shapings.

SLEEVES (both alike)
Cast on 25 (27: 29) sts using 4mm (US 6) needles.
Work 3 rows in garter st, ending with a RS row.
Change to 5 mm (US 8) needles and work in moss st as for back, shaping sides by inc 1 st at each end of 4th and every foll 4th row to 39 (37: 47) sts, then on every foll 6th row until there are 41 (45: 51) sts, taking inc sts into patt.
Cont without further shaping until sleeve measures 14.5 (18.5: 20) cm, ending with a WS row.
Cast off evenly.

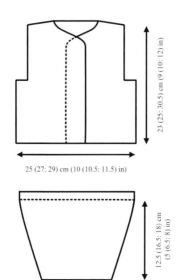

25 (27: 29) cm (10 (10.5: 11.5) in)

23 (25: 30.5) cm (9 (10: 12) in)

12.5 (16.5: 18) cm (5 (6.5: 8) in)

MAKING UP
PRESS all pieces as described on the info page.
Join shoulder seams using back stitch.
Set sleeve into armhole using the square set-in method described on the information page.
Sew on button to correspond with buttonhole in right front.
See information page for finishing instructions.

Design number 24

Squiffy

YARN
Rowan D.K. Soft

A	Flushed	172	1	x	50gm
B	Luna	173	1	x	50gm
C	Tawny	171	1	x	50gm

NEEDLES
1 pair 3¾ mm (no 9) (US 5) needles

TENSION
23 sts and 36 rows to 10 cm measured over st st using 3¾mm (US 5) needles.

MEASUREMENTS
Finished scarf is approx 22.5 cm (9 in) wide by 170 cm (67 in) long.

SCARF
Cast on 52 sts using 3¾ mm (US 5) needles and yarn A.
Work 4 rows in garter st, ending with a WS row.
Cont with yarn A and, beg with a K row, work 14 rows in st st.
Change to yarn B and work a further 14 rows in st st.
Change to yarn C and work a further 14 rows in st st.
Last 42 rows form striped st st patt and are rep throughout.
Cont straight until work measures approx169 cm from cast-on edge, ending with 14 rows st st in yarn A.
Cont with yarn A, work 3 rows in garter st, ending with a RS row.
Cast off evenly knitwise (on WS).

Design number 25

Scamp

YARN

3rd	4th	5th	6th	7th	8th	9th	
To fit							
1-2	2-3	3-4	4-5	6-7	8-9	9-10 yrs	
Chest size							
20	22	23	24	26	28	30	in
(51	56	58	61	66	71	76	cm)

Crew neck sweater
Rowan Handknit Cotton DK
(photographed in Raindrop 206)

5	7	8	9	10	12	14	x 50gm

Rowan Denim

6	7	8	10	11	13	15	x 50 gm

Collared sweater
Rowan Handknit Cotton DK

6	8	9	10	12	14	16	x 50 gm

Rowan Denim
(photographed in Nashville 225)

7	8	9	11	13	15	17	x 50 gm

NEEDLES

1 pair 3¼mm (no 10) (US 3) needles
1 pair 4mm (no 8) (US 6) needles

BUTTONS - 2 for Collared sweater
7.5 cm of velcro for Collared sweater

TENSION

Handknit DK Cotton: 20 sts and 28 rows to
10 cm measured over stocking stitch using 4mm
(US 6) needles.
Denim: Before washing 20 sts and 28 rows to
10 cm measured over stocking stitch using 4mm
(US 6) needles.

Tension note: Denim will shrink in length
when washed for the first time. Allowances have
been made in this pattern for shrinkage (see size
diagram for after washing measurements).

BACK

Cast on 67 (75: 81: 87: 93: 101: 111) sts using
3¼mm (US 3) needles.
Beg with a K row, work 6 rows in st st.
Starting and ending rows as indicated and rep
rows 1 to 8 **only**, cont in patt from chart as folls:
Work 6 (6: 6: 6: 8: 8: 8) rows.
Change to 4mm (US 6) needles.
Handknit DK Cotton version
Cont straight until back measures approx
16 (18.5: 22.5: 24: 26.5: 30.5: 33) cm from lower
edge, allowing first 6 rows to roll to RS and
ending with chart row 8.
Denim version
Cont straight until back measures approx
19.5 (22.5: 27.5: 29: 32: 37: 40) cm from lower
edge, allowing first 6 rows to roll to RS and
ending with chart row 8.
Both versions
Work chart rows 9 to 14, ending with a WS row.
Shape armholes
Keeping chart correct, cast off 4 (5: 5: 5: 6: 6: 6) sts
at beg of next 2 rows.
59 (65: 71: 77: 81: 89: 99) sts.★★
Work chart rows 17 to 36 and then repeat chart
rows 15 to 36 **only**, cont as folls:
Handknit DK Cotton version
Cont straight until armhole measures 14 (15.5:
16.5: 18: 19: 20.5: 22) cm, ending with a WS row.
Denim version
Cont straight until armhole measures 17 (19: 20:
22: 23: 25: 26.5) cm, ending with a WS row.
Both versions
Shape shoulders and back neck
Next row (RS): Patt until there are 21 (23: 26:
28: 29: 32: 36) sts on right needle and turn,
leaving rem sts on a holder.
Work each side of neck separately.
Cast off 4 sts at beg of next row.
Cast off rem 17 (19: 22: 24: 25: 28: 32) sts.
With RS facing, rejoin yarn to rem sts, cast off
centre 17 (19: 19: 21: 23: 25: 27) sts, patt to end.
Work to match first side, reversing shapings.

CREW NECK SWEATER FRONT

Work as for back until 12 (12: 14: 14: 16: 16: 18)
rows less have been worked than on back to
shoulder cast-off, ending with a WS row.
Shape neck
Next row (RS): Patt 24 (26: 30: 32: 34: 37: 42)
sts and turn, leaving rem sts on a holder.
Work each side of neck separately.
Cast off 4 sts at beg of next row.
Dec 1 st at neck edge of next 3 rows, then on
foll 0 (0: 1: 1: 2: 2: 3) alt rows.
17 (19: 22: 24: 25: 28: 32) sts.
Work 7 rows.
Shape shoulder
Cast off rem 17 (19: 22: 24: 25: 28: 32) sts.
With RS facing, rejoin yarn to rem sts, cast off
centre 11 (13: 11: 13: 13: 15: 15) sts, patt to end.
Work to match first side, reversing shapings.

COLLARED SWEATER POCKET LINING

Cast on 49 (51: 53: 55: 57: 59: 61) sts using 4mm
(US 6) needles.
Handknit DK Cotton version
Beg with a K row, work 12 (12.5: 12.5: 14: 14:
16: 16) cm in st st, ending a RS row.
Denim version
Beg with a K row, work 14 (15: 15: 17: 17: 19: 19)
cm in st st, ending a RS row.
Both versions
Break yarn and leave sts on a holder.

COLLARED SWEATER FRONT

Work as for back to ★★.
Keeping patt correct as for back, cont as folls:
Work 2 rows.
Place pocket
Next row (RS): Patt 5 (7: 9: 11: 12: 15: 19) sts,
cast off next 49 (51: 53: 55: 57: 59: 61) sts in patt,
patt to end.
Next row: Patt 5 (7: 9: 11: 12: 15: 19) sts, with
WS facing now patt across 49 (51: 53: 55: 57: 59:
61) sts of pocket lining, patt to end.
Handknit DK Cotton version
Cont in patt until armhole measures 7.5 (8: 8: 9:
10: 11: 11) cm, ending with a WS row.
Denim version
Cont in patt until armhole measures 9 (10: 10:
11: 12: 13: 13) cm, ending with a WS row.
Both versions
Divide for front opening
Next row (RS): Patt 27 (30: 33: 36: 38: 42: 47)
sts, [K1, P1] twice, K1 and turn, leaving rem sts
on a holder. 32 (35: 38: 41: 43: 47: 52) sts.
Work each side of neck separately.
Next row: K1, [P1, K1] twice, patt to end.
Last 2 rows set position of 5 st front opening
border worked in moss st.
Keeping border and patt correct, cont as folls:
Cont straight until 10 (10: 12: 12: 14: 14: 16)
rows less have been worked than on back to
shoulder cast-off, ending with a WS row.
Shape neck
Next row (RS): Patt 24 (26: 30: 32: 34: 37: 42) sts
and turn, leaving rem 8 (9: 8: 9: 9: 10: 10) sts on
a holder.
Cast off 4 sts at beg of next row.
Dec 1 st at neck edge of next 3 rows, then on
foll 0 (0: 1: 1: 2: 2: 3) alt rows.
17 (19: 22: 24: 25: 28: 32) sts.
Work 5 rows.
Shape shoulder
Cast off rem 17 (19: 22: 24: 25: 28: 32) sts.
With RS facing, rejoin yarn to rem sts and cont
as folls:
Next row (RS): Cast on 5 sts, work across these
5 sts as folls: [K1, P1] twice, K1, patt to end.
Next row: Patt to last 5 sts, K1, [P1, K1] twice.
Last 2 rows set position of 5 st front opening
border worked in moss st.
Keeping border and patt correct, cont as folls:
Cont straight until 10 (10: 12: 12: 14: 14: 16)
rows less have been worked than on back to
shoulder cast-off, ending with a WS row.
Shape neck
Next row (RS): Patt 8 (9: 8: 9: 9: 10: 10) sts and
slip these sts onto a holder, patt to end.
24 (26: 30: 32: 34: 37: 42) sts.
Work 1 row. Cast off 4 sts at beg of next row.
Dec 1 st at neck edge of next 3 rows, then on
foll 0 (0: 1: 1: 2: 2: 3) alt rows.
17 (19: 22: 24: 25: 28: 32) sts.
Work 5 rows.
Shape shoulder
Cast off rem 17 (19: 22: 24: 25: 28: 32) sts.

SLEEVES (both alike)

Cast on 35 (39: 41: 43: 47: 49: 51) sts using 3¼mm (US 3) needles.

Beg with a K row, work 6 rows in st st.
Starting and ending rows as indicated and repeating rows 1 to 8 **only** throughout, cont in patt from chart as folls:
Work 4 rows.
Change to 4mm (US 6) needles.

Handknit DK Cotton version

Inc 1 st at each end of next and every foll 4th (4th: 4th: 4th: 6th: 6th: 6th) row to 51 (65: 69: 75: 59: 59: 61) sts, then on every foll alt (alt: alt: alt: 4th: 4th: 4th) row until there are 61 (67: 71: 77: 81: 87: 93) sts, taking inc sts into patt.
Cont straight until sleeve measures 20 (24: 25.5: 28.5: 33.5: 36: 38.5) cm from lower edge, allowing first 6 rows to roll to RS and ending with a WS row.

Denim version

Inc 1 st at each end of next and every foll 4th (6th: 6th: 6th: 6th: 6th: 6th) row to 57 (47: 53: 57: 75: 77: 79) sts, then on every foll alt (4th: 4th: 4th: 4th: 4th: 4th) row until there are 61 (67: 71: 77: 81: 87: 93) sts, taking inc sts into patt.
Cont straight until sleeve measures 24 (29: 30.5: 34: 40: 43: 46) cm from lower edge, allowing first 6 rows to roll to RS and ending with a WS row.

Both versions

Cast off loosely.

MAKING UP

PRESS all pieces as described on the information page.

Crew neck sweater only

Join right shoulder seam using back stitch.

Neck border

With RS facing and 3¼mm (US 3) needles, pick up and knit 15 (15: 17: 17: 19: 19: 21) sts down left front neck, 11 (13: 11: 13: 13: 15: 15) sts across front neck, 15 (15: 17: 17: 19: 19: 21) sts up right front neck, and 25 (27: 27: 29: 31: 33: 35) sts across back neck.
66 (70: 72: 76: 82: 86: 92) sts.

Handknit DK Cotton version

Beg with a P row, work 11 rows in st st.

Denim version

Beg with a P row, work 13 rows in st st.

Both versions

Cast off loosely knitwise.
Join left shoulder and neck border seam using back stitch, reversing seam for st st roll.

Collared sweater only

Join shoulder seams using back stitch.

Collar

With RS facing and 3¼mm (US 3) needles, slip 8 (9: 8: 9: 9: 10: 10) sts from right front holder onto right needle, rejoin yarn and pick up and knit 15 (15: 17: 17: 19: 19: 21) sts up right front neck, 25 (27: 27: 29: 31: 33: 35) sts across back neck, and 15 (15: 17: 17: 19: 19: 21) sts down left front neck, then patt across 8 (9: 8: 9: 9: 10: 10) sts from left front holder.
71 (75: 77: 81: 87: 91: 97) sts.

Handknit DK Cotton version

Work 7 (7: 7.5: 7.5: 8.5: 8.5: 8.5) cm in moss st as set by front borders.

Denim version

Work 8 (8: 9: 9: 10: 10: 10) cm in moss st as set by front borders.

Both versions

Cast off loosely and evenly in moss st.

Pocket flap

Cast on 51 (53: 55: 57: 59: 61: 63) sts using 4mm (US 6) needles.
1st row (RS): K1, *P1, K1, rep from * to end.
Keeping moss st correct as set by last row, cont as folls:
Work 5 rows.
Buttonhole row (RS): Moss st 4, cast off 2 sts, moss st to last 6 sts, cast off 2 sts, moss st to end.
Next row: Moss st to end, casting on 2 sts over those cast off on previous row.
Work 8 (8: 8: 10: 10: 10: 10) rows.
Cast off in patt.
Sew pocket flap to front above pocket opening as in photograph. Sew on buttons. Attach velcro to pocket flap and pocket front halfway between buttons to prevent sagging.

Both versions

See information page for finishing instructions, setting in sleeves using the square set-in method.

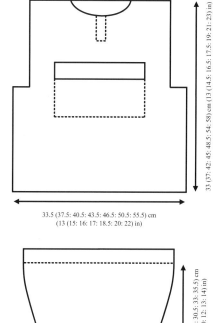

33.5 (37.5: 40.5: 43.5: 46.5: 50.5: 55.5) cm
(13 (15: 16: 17: 18.5: 20: 22) in)

33 (37: 42: 45: 48.5: 54: 58) cm (13 (14.5: 16.5: 17.5: 19: 21: 23) in)

18 (21.5: 23: 26: 30.5: 33: 35.5) cm
(7 (8.5: 9: 10: 12: 13: 14) in)

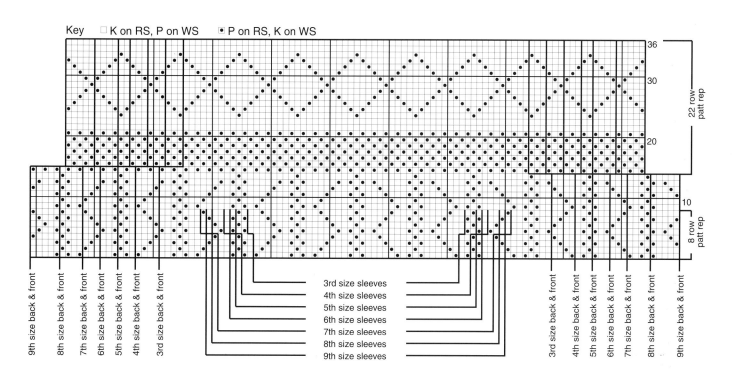

Key □ K on RS, P on WS   ▣ P on RS, K on WS

36
30
22 row patt rep
20
10
8 row patt rep

9th size back & front
8th size back & front
7th size back & front
6th size back & front
5th size back & front
4th size back & front
3rd size back & front

3rd size sleeves
4th size sleeves
5th size sleeves
6th size sleeves
7th size sleeves
8th size sleeves
9th size sleeves

3rd size back & front
4th size back & front
5th size back & front
6th size back & front
7th size back & front
8th size back & front
9th size back & front

75

Twinkle

YARN

Rowan 4 ply Cotton

	6th	7th	8th	9th
To fit	4-5 yrs	6-7 yrs	8-9 yrs	9-10 yrs
Chest size	24	26	28	30 in
	(61	66	71	76 cm)
	5	6	7	8 x 50 gm

(photographed in Black 101)

NEEDLES

1 pair 2¼ mm (no 13) (US 1) needles
1 pair 3 mm (no 11) (US 2/3) needles

BUTTONS

7

BEADS

approx 1300 (1450: 1600: 1650) small gold beads

TENSION

28 sts and 36 rows to 10 cm measured over st st using 3 mm (US 2/3) needles.

Pattern note

Bead work - the bead positions are marked by symbols on the chart. First thread required number of beads onto the yarn. Knit to the position of the bead, bring the yarn forward to RS of work, then slide the bead down close to the last stitch worked, slip the next stitch from the left hand needle purlwise, pass the bead in front of the slipped stitch tightly, then take the yarn to the back and knit the next stitch, leaving the bead sitting in front of the slipped stitch. Do not place a bead on end sts of rows.

BACK

Cast on 93 (101: 113: 119) sts using 2¼ mm (US 1) needles.
Row 1 (RS) : K1, ★ P1, K1, rep from ★ to end.
Row 2 : As row 1.
These 2 rows form moss st.
Work a further 4 rows in moss st.
Change to 3 mm (US 2/3) needles and work 2 rows in st st, beg with a K row.
Beg and ending rows as indicated, cont in patt from chart A, placing beads as indicated, until

9 rows have been completed, inc 1 st at each end of 3rd row. 95 (103: 115: 121) sts.
Beg with a P row, cont in st st, inc 1 st at each end of 8th and every foll 14th row until there are 99 (109: 121: 127) sts.
Cont straight until back measures 15 (17: 19: 20) cm from cast-on edge, ending with a WS row.
Cont in patt from chart B, placing beads as indicated, until chart row 12 has been completed.

Shape armholes

Keeping patt correct, cast off 4 sts at beg of next 2 rows. 91 (101: 113: 119) sts.
Work 4 rows, dec 1st at each end of every row. 83 (93: 105: 111) sts.
Cont in patt from chart, rep the 8 row patt rep throughout, and AT THE SAME TIME cont to shape armholes by dec st at each end of every row until 79 (87: 93: 99) sts rem.
Cont straight until armhole measures 17 (18: 19: 20) cm, ending with a WS row.

Shape shoulders and back neck

Cast off 8 (9: 9: 10) sts at beg of next 2 rows. 63 (69: 75: 79) sts.
Next row (RS): Cast off 8 (9: 9: 10) sts, patt until there are 12 (12: 14: 14) sts on right needle and turn, leaving rem sts on a holder.
Work each side of neck separately.
Cast off 4 sts at beg of next row.
Cast off rem 8 (8: 10: 10) sts.
With RS facing, rejoin yarn to rem sts, cast off centre 23 (27: 29: 31) sts, patt to end.
Work to match first side, reversing shaping.

LEFT FRONT

Cast on 53 (57: 63: 65) sts using 2¼ mm (US 1) needles and work 5 rows in moss st as given for back, ending with a RS row.
Next row (WS): Moss st 6, slip these sts onto a holder for button border, moss st to last 0 (0: 0: 1) st, (inc in last st) 0 (0: 0: 1) time.
47 (51: 57: 60) sts.
Change to 3 mm (US 2/3) needles and work 2 rows in st st, beg with a K row.
Beg and ending rows as indicated, cont in patt from chart A, placing beads as indicated, until 9 rows have been completed, inc 1 st at beg of 3rd row. 48 (52: 58: 61) sts.
Beg with a P row, cont in st st, inc 1 st at beg of 8th and every foll 14th row until there are 50 (55: 61: 64) sts.
Cont straight until left front matches back to beg of chart B, ending with a WS row.
Cont in patt from chart B, placing beads as indicated, until chart row 12 has been completed.

Shape armholes

Keeping patt correct, cast off 4 sts at beg of next row. 46 (51: 57: 60) sts.
Work 1 row.
Work 4 rows, dec 1 st at armhole edge of every row. 42 (47: 53: 56) sts.
Cont in patt from chart, rep the 8 row patt rep throughout, and AT THE SAME TIME cont to shape armhole by dec 1 st at armhole edge of every row until 40 (44: 47: 50) sts rem.
Cont straight until left front is 13 (17: 19: 21) rows shorter than back to start of shoulder shaping, ending with a RS row.

Shape neck

Cast off 8 sts at beg of next row, and 4 sts at beg of foll alt row.
28 (32: 35: 38) sts.
Dec 1 st at neck edge on next 3 rows, then on every foll alt row until 24 (27: 29: 31) sts rem.

7th, 8th & 9th sizes only

Dec 1 st at neck edge on foll 4th row.
– (26: 28: 30) sts.

All sizes

Work 5 (3: 3: 3) rows straight, ending with a WS row.

Shape shoulder

Cast off 8 (9: 9: 10) sts at beg of next and foll alt row.
Work 1 row.
Cast off rem 8 (8: 10: 10) sts.

RIGHT FRONT

Cast on 53 (57: 63: 65) sts using 2¼ mm (US 1) needles and work 5 rows in moss st as given for back, ending with a RS row.
Next row (WS): (Inc in first st) 0 (0: 0: 1) time, moss st to last 6 sts and turn, leaving rem 6 sts on a holder for buttonhole border. 47 (51: 57: 60) sts.
Change to 3 mm (US 2/3) needles and work 2 rows in st st, beg with a K row.
Beg and ending rows as indicated, cont in patt from chart A, placing beads as indicated, until 9 rows have been completed, inc 1 st at end of 3rd row. 48 (52: 58: 61) sts.
Complete to match left front, reversing all shaping.

SLEEVES

Cast on 47 (51: 53: 57) sts using 2¼ mm (US 1) needles and work 6 rows in moss st as given for back.
Change to 3 mm (US 2/3) needles and work 2 rows in st st, beg with a K row.
Beg and ending rows as indicated, cont in patt from chart A, placing beads as indicated, until 9 rows have been completed, inc 1 st at each end of 1st and 7th rows. 51 (55: 57: 61) sts.
Beg with a P row, cont in st st, inc 1 st at each end of 4th and every foll 6th row until there are 53 (69: 75: 79) sts, then on every 4th row to 95 (101: 107: 113) sts.
Cont without further shaping until sleeve measures 29.5 (33.5: 37: 40.5) cm, ending with a WS row.

Shape top

Cast off 4 sts at beg of next 2 rows.
87 (93: 99: 105) sts.
Dec 1 st at each end of next and every alt row to 77 (81: 83: 89) sts.
Work 1 row.
Cast off evenly.

MAKING UP

PRESS all pieces as described on the information page.
Join both shoulder seams using back stitch.

Button border

Slip sts from left front holder onto 2¼ mm (US 1) needles and rejoin yarn with RS facing. Cont in moss st as set until border, when slightly stretched, fits up left front opening edge to neck shaping, ending with a WS row.
Cast off in moss st.
Slip st border in place.
Mark positions for 7 buttons on this border - the first button to come immediately after moss st border, last button 1 cm below neck shaping and rem 5 buttons evenly spaced between.

Buttonhole border

Work as for button border, rejoining yarn with WS facing and with the addition of 7 buttonholes to correspond with positions marked for buttons, worked as folls:

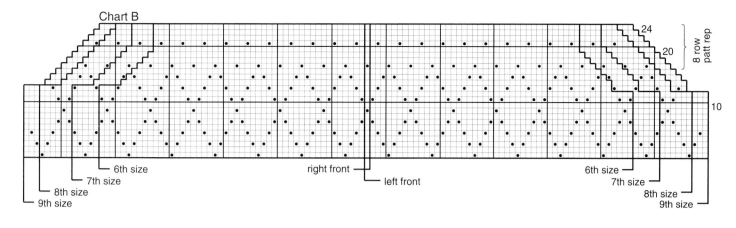

Chart B

Chart A Key ☐ K on RS rows, P on WS rows ● Place bead

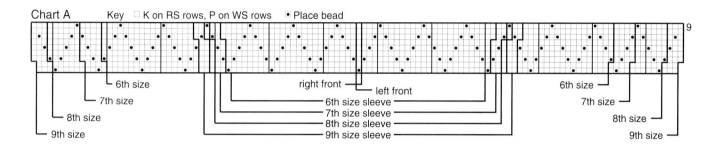

Buttonhole row (RS): Moss st 2, yon, patt 2tog, moss st 2.

Slip st border in place.

Collar

With RS facing and using 2¼ mm (US 1) needles, starting and ending midway across top of bands, pick up and knit 29 (33: 34: 36) sts up right side of neck, 31 (35: 37: 39) sts from back, and 29 (33: 34: 36) sts down left side of neck. 89 (101: 105: 111) sts.

Work 6 (7: 7: 8) cm in moss st as for back.

Cast off evenly in moss st.

Set sleeve into armhole using the shallow set-in method described on the information page.

Sew on buttons to correspond with buttonholes.

See information page for finishing instructions.

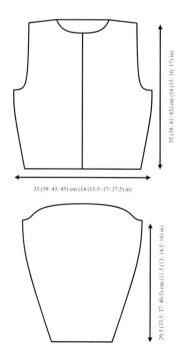

Design number 27

Mushroom

YARN

Rowan All Seasons Cotton

2 x 50gm

Oddment of same yarn in contrast for embroidery

(photographed in Jersey 191 trimmed with Mocha 193)

NEEDLES

1 pair 3¼mm (no 10) (US 3) needles

1 pair 4mm (no 8) (US 6) needles

BUTTONS - 1

TENSION

18 sts and 36 rows to 10 cm measured over garter st using 4mm (US 6) needles.

BAG

Cast on 37 sts using 4mm (US 6) needles and, beg with a RS row, cont in garter st until work measures 42 cm from cast-on edge.

Cast off evenly.

STRAP

Cast on 7 sts using 3¼mm (US 3) needles and cont in garter st until work measures approx 70 cm.

Cast off firmly.

MAKING UP

Press all pieces as described on the information page.

Turn up approx 15 cm from cast-on edge to form body of bag and oversew edges firmly, using contrast yarn.

Fold over approx 8 cm from cast-off edge to form flap and, using photograph as a guide, oversew edges for decoration.

Top stitch ends of strap in place on reverse of bag.

Make button loop using 3¼mm needles as folls: using the cable cast-on method, cast on 22 sts. Cast off evenly.

Fold button loop in half and neatly stitch in place on flap of bag.

Sew on button to correspond with button loop.

Design number 28

Fletcher

YARN

Rowan All Seasons Cotton

	4th	5th	6th	7th	8th	9th
To fit	2-3	3-4	4-5	6-7	8-9	9-10 yrs
Chest size	22	23	24	26	28	30 in
	(56	58	61	66	71	76 cm)
	6	7	8	10	11	13 x 50 gm

(photographed in Orkney 196 and Mellow 190)

NEEDLES

1 pair 4mm (no 8) (US 6) needles
1 pair 5mm (no 6) (US 8) needles

TENSION

17 sts and 24 rows to 10 cm measured over pattern using 5mm (US 8) needles.

BACK

Cast on 63 (69: 73: 79: 85: 95) sts using 4mm (US 6) needles.
Knit 4 (4: 4: 6: 6: 6) rows, ending with a WS row.
Change to 5mm (US 8) needles.
Beg with a K row, work 2 rows in st st from chart A.
Starting and ending rows as indicated, cont to work from chart A until 18 rows have been completed.
Cont in patt from chart A, repeat the 8 row patt rep until work measures 17.5 (21: 22: 25: 28: 29) cm, ending with a **RS** row.
Next row (WS): Purl.
Now cont from chart B, work 6 (8: 10: 12: 16: 18) rows straight, ending with a WS row.
Shape armholes
Keeping patt correct, cast off 4 (4: 4: 5: 5: 5) sts at beg of next 2 rows. 55 (61: 65: 69: 75: 85) sts.
Cont in patt, repeat the 30 patt rows as indicated until armhole measures 16.5 (17.5: 19: 20: 21.5: 23) cm, ending with a WS row.
Shape shoulders and back neck
Cast off 5 (6: 7: 7: 8: 9) sts at beg of next 2 rows. 45 (49: 51: 55: 59: 67) sts.
Next row (RS): Cast off 5 (6: 7: 7: 8: 9) sts, patt until there are 10 (11: 10: 11: 11: 13) sts on right needle and turn, leaving rem sts on a holder.
Work each side of neck separately.
Cast off 4 sts at beg of next row.
Cast off rem 6 (7: 6: 7: 7: 9) sts.
With RS facing, rejoin yarn to rem sts, cast off centre 15 (15: 17: 19: 21: 23) sts, patt to end.
Work to match first side, reversing shapings.

FRONT

Cast on 63 (69: 73: 79: 85: 95) sts using 4mm (US 6) needles.
Knit 4 (4: 4: 6: 6: 6) rows, ending with a WS row.
Change to 5mm (US 8) needles.
Beg with a K row, work 2 rows in st st from chart A.
Starting and ending rows as indicated and keeping patt correct as for back, now work in patt from chart A as folls:
Work 4 (4: 4: 8: 8: 8) rows, ending with a WS row.
Place pocket
Next row (RS): Patt 14 (17: 19: 14: 17: 22) sts, slip next 35 (35: 35: 51: 51: 51) sts onto a holder, turn, cast on 35 (35: 35: 51: 51: 51) sts, turn and patt rem 14 (17: 19: 14: 17: 22) sts of row.
Patt 25 (25: 25: 33: 33: 33) rows, ending with a WS row.
Do NOT break yarn but set these sts aside.
Work pocket front
Slip 35 (35: 35: 51: 51: 51) sts left on a holder onto 5mm (US 8) needles and rejoin yarn with RS facing.
Next row (RS): K3, patt to last 3 sts, K3.
Next row: K3, patt to last 3 sts, K3.
Rep last 2 rows 12 (12: 12: 16: 16: 16) times more, ending with a WS row. Break yarn.
Join sections
Return to first set of sts and cont as folls:
Next row (RS): Patt first 14 (17: 19: 14: 17: 22) sts of main section, then holding pocket front sts against main section, work tog first st of pocket front with next st of main section, cont across rem 34 (34: 34: 50: 50: 50) sts of pocket front and main section in same way, then patt rem 14 (17: 19: 14: 17: 22) sts of main section.
Cont straight until front matches back to beg of armhole shaping, ending with a WS row.
Shape armholes
Keeping chart correct, cast off 4 (4: 4: 5: 5: 5) sts at beg of next 2 rows. 55 (61: 65: 69: 75: 85) sts.
Cont in patt until 10 (10: 10: 12: 12: 14) rows less have been worked than on back to start of shoulder shaping, ending with a WS row.
Divide for front opening
Next row (RS): Patt 26 (29: 31: 33: 36: 41) sts, K3 and turn, leaving rem sts on a holder.
29 (32: 34: 36: 39: 44) sts.

Work each side of neck separately.
Next row: K3, patt to end.
Last 2 rows set position of front opening border 3 sts worked as K sts on every row.
Keeping border and patt correct, cont straight until front matches back to start of shoulder shaping, ending with a WS row.
Shape shoulder
Cast off 5 (6: 7: 7: 8: 9) sts at beg of next and foll alt row, then 6 (7: 6: 7: 7: 9) sts at beg of foll alt row.
Work 1 row.
Break yarn and leave rem 13 (13: 14: 15: 16: 17) sts on a holder.
With RS facing, rejoin yarn to rem sts and cont as folls:
Next row (RS): Cast on and K 3 sts, patt to end.
29 (32: 34: 36: 39: 44) sts.
Next row: Patt to last 3 sts, K3.
Last 2 rows set position of front opening border 3 sts worked as K sts on every row.
Keeping border and patt correct, cont straight until front matches back to start of shoulder shaping, ending with a RS row.
Shape shoulder
Cast off 5 (6: 7: 7: 8: 9) sts at beg of next and foll alt row, then 6 (7: 6: 7: 7: 9) sts at beg of foll alt row.
Do NOT break yarn.
Leave rem 13 (13: 14: 15: 16: 17) sts on a holder and set aside ball of yarn - this will be used for hood.

SLEEVES (both alike)
Cast on 33 (35: 37: 39: 41: 43) sts using 4mm (US 6) needles.
Knit 4 (4: 4: 6: 6: 6) rows, ending with a WS row.
Change to 5mm (US 8) needles.
Beg with a K row, work 2 rows in st st from chart A.
Starting and ending rows as indicated, cont in patt from chart A, at the same time shaping sides by inc 1 st at each end of next and every foll 4th row until there are 57 (59: 65: 69: 73: 79) sts, taking inc sts into patt.
Cont straight until sleeve measures 24 (25.5: 28.5: 33.5: 36: 38.5) cm from cast-on edge, ending with a WS row.
Cast off loosely.

MAKING UP
PRESS all pieces as described on the information page.
Join shoulder seams using back stitch.
Hood
With RS facing, using ball of yarn left at right front neck edge and 5mm (US 8) needles, K across 13 (13: 14: 15: 16: 17) sts of right front, pick up and knit 24 (24: 26: 28: 30: 32) sts across back neck placing markers on centre 2 sts, then K across 13 (13: 14: 15: 16: 17) sts of left front. 50 (50: 54: 58: 62: 66) sts.
Next row (WS): K3, P to last 3 sts, K3.
Next row: K5, starting with row 1, work across 9 sts from chart C, K to marked sts, M1, K2 marked sts, M1, K to last 14 sts, work across 9 sts from chart C, K5.
Next row: K3, P2, work across row 2 from chart C, P to last 14 sts, work across row 2 from chart C, P2, K3.
Keeping patt from chart C correct, cont to work in st st with 3 border sts in garter st, inc 1 st at each side of centre back 2 sts as before on every foll 4th row until there are 62 (62: 66: 70: 74: 78) sts.
Cont straight until hood measures 23.5 (23.5: 26.5: 26.5: 30: 30) cm, ending with a WS row.

Chart C

8 row patt rep

Chart B

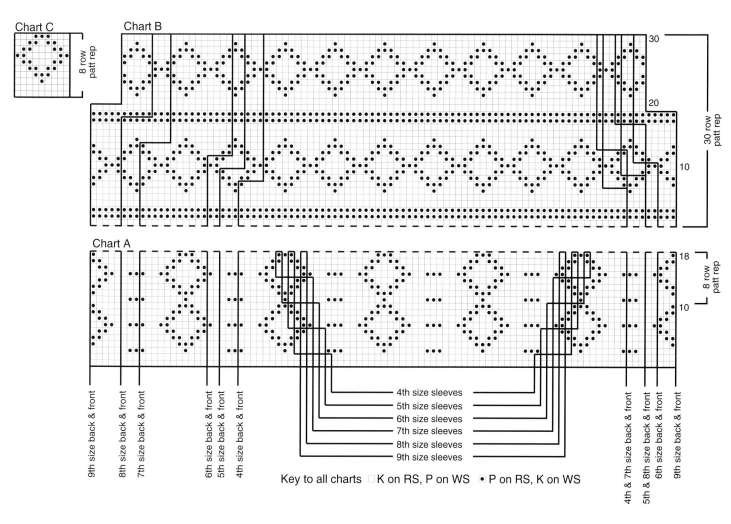

30 row patt rep

30
20
10

Chart A

8 row patt rep

18
10

9th size back & front
8th size back & front
7th size back & front
6th size back & front
5th size back & front
4th size back & front

4th size sleeves
5th size sleeves
6th size sleeves
7th size sleeves
8th size sleeves
9th size sleeves

4th & 7th size back & front
5th & 8th size back & front
6th size back & front
9th size back & front

Key to all charts ☐ K on RS, P on WS ● P on RS, K on WS

Next row (RS) (dec): Patt to within 2 sts of marked centre back sts, K2tog, K2 marked sts, K2tog tbl, patt to end.

Work 1 row.

Rep last 2 rows 3 times more.

54 (54: 58: 62: 66: 70) sts.

Next row (RS): K27 (27: 29: 31: 33: 35) sts and turn.

Fold hood in half with RS facing and, using a spare needle, cast off sts from each needle tog to form hood seam.

Lay one front border over the other and sew cast-on edge in place on inside. Sew cast-on edge of pocket back in place on inside.

See information page for finishing instructions, setting in sleeves using the square set-in method.

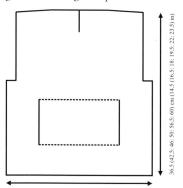

37 (40.5: 43: 46.5: 50: 56) cm (14.5 (16: 17: 18.5: 19.5: 22) in)

36.5 (42.5: 46: 50: 56.5: 60) cm (14.5 (16.5: 18: 19.5: 22: 23.5) in)

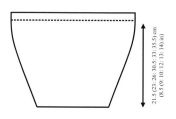

21.5 (23: 26: 30.5: 33: 35.5) cm (8.5 (9: 10: 12: 13: 14) in)

Design number 29

Peaches

YARN

Rowan Handknit D.K. Cotton

A	Raindrop	206	2	x 50gm
B	Fruit Salad	203	1	x 50gm
C	Soft Green	228	1	x 50gm
D	Rose	208	1	x 50gm
E	Gerba	223	2	x 50gm

NEEDLES

1 pair 3¼mm (no 10) (US 3) needles
1 pair 4mm (no 8) (US 6) needles

TENSION

20 sts and 28 rows to 10 cm measured over st st using 4mm (US 6) needles.

MEASUREMENTS

Finished blanket is approx 54 cm (21 in) wide by 71 cm (28 in) long.

BLANKET

Cast on 108 sts using 3¼mm (US 3) needles and yarn A.

Work 10 rows in garter st, ending with a WS row.

Change to 4mm (US 6) needles and, joining-in and breaking-off colours as required, cont in patt as folls:

Row 1 (RS): Using yarn A, K.

Row 2: Using yarn A, K6, P to last 6 sts, K6.

These 2 rows set the stitches.

Keeping 6 sts at both sides in garter st as set, work a further 10 rows in yarn A.

Change to yarn B and work 12 rows in patt.

Change to yarn C and work 12 rows in patt.

Change to yarn D and work 12 rows in patt.

Change to yarn E and work 12 rows in patt.

Rep these 60 rows twice more, ending with 12 rows patt in yarn E.

Change to 3¼mm (US 3) needles and, cont with yarn E, work 9 rows in garter st, ending with a RS row.

Cast off evenly knitwise (on WS).

Design number 30

Action

YARN
Rowan Handknit Cotton DK

	4th	5th	6th	7th	8th	9th	
To fit							
	2-3	3-4	4-5	6-7	8-9	9-10	yrs
Chest size							
	22	23	24	26	28	30	in
	(56	58	61	66	71	76	cm)
	7	8	10	11	13	15	x 50 gm

(photographed in Bleached 263 and Artichoke 209)

NEEDLES
1 pair 3¼mm (no 10) (US 3) needles
1 pair 4mm (no 8) (US 6) needles

TENSION
20 sts and 28 rows to 10 cm measured over pattern using 4mm (US 6) needles.

BACK
Cast on 75 (81: 87: 93: 101: 111) sts using 3¼mm (US 3) needles.
Beg with a K row, work 4 (4: 4: 6: 6: 6) rows in st st.
Change to 4mm (US 6) needles and work in moss st as folls:
Row 1 (RS): K0 (1: 0: 1: 1: 0), ★P1, K1, rep from ★ to last 1 (0: 1: 0: 0: 1) st, P1 (0: 1: 0: 0: 1).
Row 2: As row 1.
Work a further 6 (6: 8: 10: 12: 12) rows in moss st, ending with a WS row.
Starting and ending rows as indicated, working rows 1 to 24 and then repeating 18 row patt rep **only**, cont in patt from chart as folls:
Work straight until back measures 20.5 (23: 24: 26: 29: 32.5) cm from lower edge **allowing st st rows to roll to RS**, ending with a WS row.
Shape armholes
Keeping chart correct, cast off 5 (5: 5: 6: 6: 6) sts at beg of next 2 rows. 65 (71: 77: 81: 89: 99) sts.
Cont straight until armhole measures 16.5 (17.5: 19: 20: 21.5: 23) cm, ending with a WS row.
Shape shoulders and back neck
Cast off 6 (7: 8: 8: 9: 10) sts at beg of next 2 rows. 53 (57: 61: 65: 71: 79) sts.
Next row (RS): Cast off 6 (7: 8: 8: 9: 10) sts, patt until there are 11 (11: 11: 12: 13: 15) sts on right needle and turn, leaving rem sts on a holder.
Work each side of neck separately.
Cast off 4 sts at beg of next row.
Cast off rem 7 (7: 7: 8: 9: 11) sts.
With RS facing, rejoin yarn to rem sts, cast off centre 19 (21: 23: 25: 27: 29) sts, patt to end.
Work to match first side, reversing shapings.

FRONT
Work as for back until 24 (24: 26: 26: 28: 28) rows less have been worked than on back to start of shoulder shaping, ending with a WS row.
Shape neck
Next row (RS): Patt 32 (35: 38: 40: 44: 49) sts and turn, leaving rem sts on a holder.
Work each side of neck separately.
Dec 1 st at neck edge of next 6 (8: 8: 10: 10: 12) rows, then on foll 7 (6: 7: 6: 7: 6) alt rows.
19 (21: 23: 24: 27: 31) sts.
Work 3 rows.

Shape shoulder
Cast off 6 (7: 8: 8: 9: 10) sts at beg of next and foll alt row.
Work 1 row.
Cast off rem 7 (7: 7: 8: 9: 11) sts.
With RS facing, rejoin yarn to rem sts, cast off centre st, patt to end.
Work to match first side, reversing shapings.

SLEEVES (both alike)
Cast on 39 (41: 43: 47: 49: 51) sts using 3¼mm (US 3) needles.
Beg with a K row, work 6 rows in st st.
Change to 4mm (US 6) needles and work in moss st as folls:
Row 1 (RS): K0 (1: 0: 0: 1: 0), ★P1, K1, rep from ★ to last 1 (0: 1: 1: 0: 1) st, P1 (0: 1: 1: 0: 1).
Row 2: As row 1.
Work a further 6 (6: 10: 12: 12: 12) rows in moss st inc 1 st at each end of 5th row and foll 0 (0: 4th: 6th: 6th: 6th) row, taking inc sts into moss st and ending with a WS row.
41 (43: 47: 51: 53: 55) sts.
Starting and ending rows as indicated, working rows 1 to 24 and then repeating 18 row patt rep **only**, cont in patt from chart, shaping sides by inc 1 st at each end of 3rd and every foll 4th (4th: 4th: 6th: 6th: 6th) row to 63 (67: 73: 57: 57: 59) sts, then on every foll alt (alt: alt: 4th: 4th: 4th) row until there are 67 (71: 77: 81: 87: 93) sts, taking inc sts into patt.

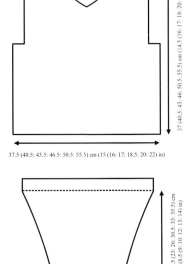

37.5 (40.5: 43.5: 46.5: 50.5: 55.5) cm (15 (16: 17: 18.5: 20: 22) in)

37 (40.5: 43: 46: 50.5: 55.5) cm (14.5 (16: 17: 18: 20: 22) in)

21.5 (23: 26: 30.5: 33: 35.5) cm (8.5 (9: 10: 12: 13: 14) in)

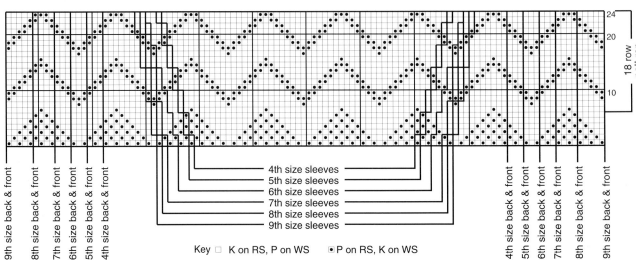

4th size sleeves
5th size sleeves
6th size sleeves
7th size sleeves
8th size sleeves
9th size sleeves

9th size back & front
8th size back & front
7th size back & front
6th size back & front
5th size back & front
4th size back & front

4th size back & front
5th size back & front
6th size back & front
7th size back & front
8th size back & front
9th size back & front

24
20
10

18 row patt rep

Key ☐ K on RS, P on WS   ▣ P on RS, K on WS

Cont straight until sleeve measures 24 (25.5: 28.5: 33.5: 36: 38.5) cm from lower edge **allowing st st rows to roll to RS**, ending with a WS row.
Cast off loosely.

MAKING UP
PRESS all pieces as described on the information page.
Join right shoulder seam using back stitch.
Neck border
With RS facing and 3¼mm (US 3) needles, pick up and knit 24 (24: 27: 27: 29: 30) sts down left front neck, 24 (24: 27: 27: 29: 30) sts up right front neck, and 27 (29: 31: 33: 35: 37) sts across back neck. 75 (77: 85: 87: 93: 97) sts.
Beg with a P row, work 5 (5: 5: 7: 7: 7) rows in st st.
Cast off loosely knitwise.
Join left shoulder and neck border seam using back stitch, reversing seam for st st roll.
See information page for finishing instructions, setting in sleeves using the square set-in method.

Design number 31

Strike

YARN
Rowan Wool Cotton

	6th	7th	8th	9th	
To fit	4-5	6-7	8-9	9-10 yrs
Chest size	24	26	28	30	in
	(61	66	71	76	cm)
	5	5	6	7 x 50gm

(photographed in Moonshine 904)

NEEDLES
1 pair 3¼mm (no 9) (US 5) needles
1 pair 4mm (no 8) (US 6) needles

TENSION
22 sts and 30 rows to 10 cm measured over stocking stitch using 4mm (US 6) needles.

BACK
Cast on 73 (79: 87: 95) sts using 3¼mm (US 5) needles.
Row 1 (RS): P2 (0: 0: 1), K3 (2: 0: 3), *P3, K3, rep from * to last 2 (5: 3: 1) sts, P2 (3: 3: 1), K0 (2: 0: 0).

Row 2: K2 (0: 0: 1), P3 (2: 0: 3), *K3, P3, rep from * to last 2 (5: 3: 1) sts, K2 (3: 3: 1), P0 (2: 0: 0).
Last 2 rows form rib.
Work a further 8 (10: 12: 14) rows in rib.
Change to 4mm (US 6) needles and, beg with a K row, cont in st st as folls:
Work 2 rows.
Next row (eyelet row) (RS): K4 (7: 4: 8), *K2tog, yfwd, K5, rep from * to last 6 (9: 6: 10) sts, K2tog, yfwd, K4 (7: 4: 8).
Cont straight until back measures 24.5 (26: 28.5: 30) cm, ending with a WS row.
Shape armholes
Cast off 4 sts at beg of next 2 rows.
65 (71: 79: 87) sts.
Dec 1 st at both ends of next 3 (3: 5: 5) rows, then on 2 foll alt rows. 55 (61: 65: 73) sts.
Cont straight until armhole measures 15 (16: 17: 18) cm, ending with a WS row.
Shape shoulders and back neck
Cast off 5 (5: 6: 7) sts at beg of next 2 rows.
45 (51: 53: 59) sts.
Next row (RS): Cast off 5 (5: 6: 7) sts, K until there are 8 (10: 9: 10) sts on right needle and turn, leaving rem sts on a holder.
Work each side of neck separately.
Cast off 4 sts at beg of next row.
Cast off rem 4 (6: 5: 6) sts.
With RS facing, rejoin yarn to rem sts, cast off centre 19 (21: 23: 25) sts, K to end.
Work to match first side, reversing shapings.

FRONT
Work as for back until 14 (14: 16: 16) rows less have been worked than on back to start of shoulder shaping, ending with a WS row.
Shape neck
Next row (RS): K21 (23: 25: 28) and turn, leaving rem sts on a holder.
Work each side of neck separately.
Dec 1 st at neck edge of next 4 rows, then on every foll alt row until 14 (16: 17: 20) sts rem.
Work 3 rows.
Shape shoulder
Cast off 5 (5: 6: 7) sts at beg of next and foll alt row.
Work 1 row.
Cast off rem 4 (6: 5: 6) sts.
With RS facing, rejoin yarn to rem sts, cast off centre 13 (15: 15: 17) sts, K to end.
Work to match first side, reversing shapings.

LEFT HOOD
Cast on 7 sts using 4mm (US 6) needles.
Row 1 (RS): K2, (P1, K1) twice, P1.
Row 2: (P1, K1) twice, P3.
These 2 rows set the stitches.
Keeping 5 sts at centre front in moss st, cont as folls:
Cast on 6 sts at beg of next and foll alt row, 5 (5: 6: 6) sts at beg of foll 3 alt rows, and 4 sts at beg of foll alt row. 38 (38: 41: 41) sts.
Work 5 rows, ending with a WS row.
Inc 1 st at beg of next and every foll 6th row until there are 44 (44: 47: 47) sts.
Cont straight until hood measures 23 (23: 24.5: 24.5) cm from last set of cast-on sts, ending with a WS row.
Dec 1 st at beg of next and foll 4th row.
42 (42: 45: 45) sts.
Work 3 rows.
Dec 1 st at shaped back edge of next 3 rows.
39 (39: 42: 42) sts.
Next row (WS): Cast off 4 sts, patt to last 2 sts, P2tog.
Dec 1 st at beg of next row.

Next row (WS): Cast off 4 sts, P to last 2 sts, P2tog.
Cast off rem 28 (28: 31: 31) sts.

RIGHT HOOD
Cast on 7 sts using 4mm (US 6) needles.
Row 1 (RS): (P1, K1) twice, P1, K2.
Row 2: Cast on and P 6 sts, P3, (K1, P1) twice.
These 2 rows set the stitches.
Keeping 5 sts at centre front in moss st, cont as folls:
Work 1 row.
Cast on 6 sts at beg of next row, 5 (5: 6: 6) sts at beg of foll 3 alt rows, and 4 sts at beg of foll alt row. 38 (38: 41: 41) sts.
Work 6 rows, ending with a WS row.
Inc 1 st at end of next and every foll 6th row until there are 44 (44: 47: 47) sts.
Cont straight until hood measures 23 (23: 24.5: 24.5) cm from last set of cast-on sts, ending with a WS row.
Dec 1 st at end of next and foll 4th row.
42 (42: 45: 45) sts.
Work 3 rows.
Dec 1 st at shaped back edge of next 2 rows.
40 (40: 43: 43) sts.
Cast off 4 sts at beg and dec 1 st at end of next row.
Dec 1 st at beg of next row.
Rep last 2 rows once more.
Cast off rem 28 (28: 31: 31) sts.

MAKING UP
PRESS all pieces as described on the information page.
Join shoulder seams using back stitch.
Armhole borders
With RS facing and 3¾mm (US 5) needles, pick up and knit 72 (78: 84: 90) sts around armhole edge.
Row 1 (WS): *K3, P3, rep from * to end.
Rep last row 3 times more, ending with a RS row.
Cast off evenly in rib.
Join back hood seam using back stitch. Sew hood to neck edge with front opening edges meeting at centre front. Make a twisted cord 120 (130: 140: 150) cm long and knot ends.
Thread through eyelet hole row as in photograph.
See information page for finishing instructions.

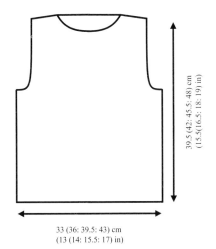

33 (36: 39.5: 43) cm
(13 (14: 15.5: 17) in)

39.5 (42: 45.5: 48) cm
(15.5 (16.5: 18: 19) in)

Cheesecake

Using the **fairisle** technique described on the info page, starting and ending rows as indicated and beg with a K row, work 10 rows in patt from chart B, which is worked entirely in st st. Beg with a K row, cont in striped st st from chart C as folls:

Cont straight until back measures 19 (20.5: 22: 24: 25) cm from cast-on edge, ending with a WS row.

Shape armholes

Cast off 3 (3: 4: 4: 4) sts at beg of next 2 rows.
70 (76: 82: 92: 98) sts.
Dec 1 st at each end of next 3 rows.
64 (70: 76: 86: 92) sts.
Cont straight until armhole measures 16 (17: 18: 19: 20) cm, ending with a WS row.

Shape shoulders and back neck

Cast off 6 (7: 7: 9: 9) sts at beg of next 2 rows.
52 (56: 62: 68: 74) sts.
Next row (RS): Cast off 6 (7: 7: 9: 9) sts, patt until there are 9 (10: 12: 12: 14) sts on right needle and turn, leaving rem sts on a holder.
Work each side of neck separately.
Cast off 4 sts at beg of next row.
Cast off rem 5 (6: 8: 8: 10) sts.
With RS facing, rejoin yarn to rem sts, cast off centre 22 (22: 24: 26: 28) sts, patt to end.
Work to match first side, reversing shapings.

LEFT FRONT
Cast on 39 (42: 46: 51: 54) sts using 2¾mm (US 2) needles and yarn H.
Beg with a K row, work in striped st st from chart A as folls:
Work 8 rows.
Change to 3¼mm (US 3) needles and cont from chart A until row 28 is complete, ending with a WS row.
Now work 10 rows in patt from chart B.
Beg with a K row, cont in striped st st from chart C as folls:
Cont straight until left front matches back to beg of armhole shaping, ending with a WS row.

Shape armholes

Cast off 3 (3: 4: 4: 4) sts at beg of next row.
36 (39: 42: 47: 50) sts.
Work 1 row.
Dec 1 st at armhole edge of next 3 rows.
33 (36: 39: 44: 47) sts.

YARN

Rowan Cotton Glace

		5th	6th	7th	8th	9th	
To fit		3-4	4-5	6-7	8-9	9-10	yrs
Chest size		23	24	26	28	30in	
		(58	61	66	71	76cm)	
A Bl Orange	445	2	2	2	2	2 x 50gm	
B Mint	748	1	2	2	2	2 x 50gm	
C Butter	795	2	2	2	2	2 x 50gm	
D Candy Fl	747	1	1	1	1	1 x 50gm	
E Hyacinth	787	1	1	2	2	2 x 50gm	
F Terracotta	786	1	1	1	1	1 x 50gm	
G Pear	780	1	1	1	1	2 x 50gm	
H Bubbles	724	2	2	2	3	3 x 50gm	

NEEDLES

1 pair 2¾mm (no 12) (US 2) needles
1 pair 3¼mm (no 10) (US 3) needles
2¾mm (no 12) (US 2) circular needle

BUTTONS - 7

TENSION

23 sts and 32 rows to 10 cm measured over stocking stitch using 3¼mm (US 3) needles.

BACK

Cast on 76 (82: 90: 100: 106) sts using 2¾mm (US 2) needles and yarn H.
Beg with a K row, work in striped st st from chart A as folls:
Work 8 rows.
Change to 3¼mm (US 3) needles and cont from chart A until row 28 has been completed, ending with a WS row.

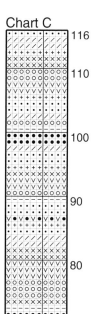

Chart A

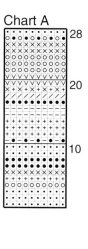

Chart C

Key

•	A
✕	B
○	C
╱	D
±	E
−	F
∨	G
▪	H

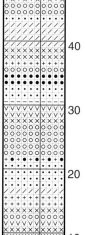

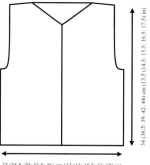

34 (36.5: 39: 42: 44) cm (13.5 (14.5: 15.5: 16.5: 17.5) in)

33 (35.5: 39: 43.5: 46) cm (13 (14: 15.5: 17: 18) in)

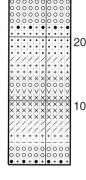

26.5 (29.5: 33.5: 37: 40.5) cm (10.5 (11.5: 13: 14.5: 16) in)

Chart B

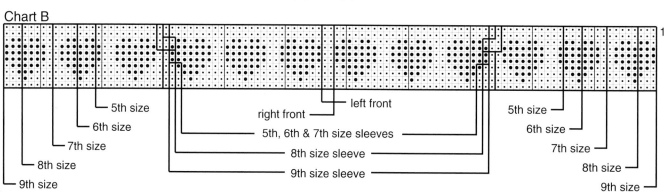

5th size
6th size
7th size
8th size
9th size
right front — left front
5th, 6th & 7th size sleeves
8th size sleeve
9th size sleeve
5th size
6th size
7th size
8th size
9th size